The Significance of Mary

The Significance of Mary

Agnes Cunningham

THE THOMAS MORE PRESS

Chicago, Illinois

ISBN 0-88347-226-0

Contents

DEDICATION

For three special women:
Helen, Cathy, Nancy

Introduction

ONE of the outcomes of the Women's Liberation Movement is the phenomenon of "women doing theology." The full impact of this development is still to be felt in the Church at large. One result of the phenomenon, however, is the growing awareness that signs and symbols, to be perennially significant, must be invested with new meanings. We need new models of discipleship, new paradigms of redemption, new names for speaking of God.

In a most particular way, the need for a new understanding of our religious symbols applies to Catholic teaching about Mary. Following the Second Council of the Vatican, a certain "disenchantment" with "devotions" came about in the Church. This was due, in part, to a renewed appreciation of the liturgy. Devotion to Mary was also affected by the feminist claim that veneration shown to the Mother of God has contributed to discrimination against women. There could be only one Mary. Thus, the rest of women are "daughters of Eve"—carrying responsibility for having brought sin and death into the world.

In 1974, Pope Paul VI promulgated *Marialis cultus,* an Apostolic Exhortation on renewal of devotion to Mary. In this document, Paul VI called our attention to Mary as a model for contemporary women and men. He asked that we set aside the idea that Mary has nothing to say to the twentieth-century disciple of Christ. He urged us to look at Mary in the light of what we have learned from studies in Scripture, historical theology and the human sciences. Paul VI asked that we take a "new look" at Mary in order to deepen our knowledge and love of her. He asked that we promote authentic devotion to her through a renewed understanding and expression of Catholic teaching about her.

To some degree, the plan I have chosen to follow for this volume is the result of the ideas to which I have just referred. The basic format actually was the outline for talks on Mary, given over the past several years. The plan is simple. I propose to present to the reader a number of "images" of Mary for consideration and reflection. In each of these images we find a unique expression of Catholic doctrine about Mary and its meaning for our participation in the life and mission of the Church today. The images I have chosen are: Our Lady of Guadalupe, the *Theotokos*, the Mother and the Child, the *Pieta* and the Woman of the Apocalypse (12:1-6). The importance of these images has been increasingly brought home to me by the responses of women with whom I have shared my ideas in workshops, conferences and parish adult education classes. In a very real way, they are the ones who have made this volume possible.

I am grateful to the Thomas More Association for the invitation to write this book, and for their willing extension

Introduction

of a challenging deadline. Of course, without Lynne Godwin, my faithful, competent secretary, the following pages might still be in a file under the label, "Current Projects."

In this Marian Year (June 7, 1987-August 15, 1988) proclaimed by Pope John Paul II, I would like to hope that this little book might contribute in some way to greater knowledge of, love for and devotion to Mary.

Agnes Cunningham

I. Mary Ever-Virgin

THE IMAGE

A RECENT television program on the Catholic Church in the United States highlighted, among other items, the growing number of Hispanic Catholics in this country. Their contribution to Catholism can be found in distinctive cultural characteristics, in deep family values and in the vitality of their religious celebrations. One of the treasures which has come to the United States with immigrants from Mexico is devotion to Our Lady of Guadalupe. In the last ten years, especially, this Marian title has been brought to the attention of Catholics across the country. Juan Diego and Castilian roses blooming in December have captured our hearts and imaginations. The "dark-skinned Mother of the poor," as she has been called, has come to be at home among us. We are drawn to know more about her and the meaning of her message for the Church today.

The story of Guadalupe is not simply a "local" tale. When the Lady appeared to Juan Diego on the rocky hilltop of Tepeyac on December 9, 1531, "Mexico" included territories that would in time come to be known as the United States. Moreover, the Lady identified herself to the Indian peasant as "the Mother of all who live united in

13

this land. . . ." Her words were echoed in the formal proclamation by Pope Pius XII, in 1945, of the Virgin of Guadalupe as Empress of All the Americas. They resounded again in the title given to her by Pope John XXIII, in 1960: Mother of the Americas. A study of the image of Our Lady of Guadalupe can help us to recognize and appreciate the inclusive, even universal, implications of this highly symbolic portrayal of Mary. In striking ways, it introduces us to some of the earliest teachings of the Church about Mary. At the same time, it calls us to recognize that every age is challenged to find new ways of thinking and speaking about Mary and her participation in the life and mission of her son.

The image of Our Lady of Guadalupe is preserved on the *tilma*, the cloak of roughly woven agave (maguey) cactus cloth worn by Juan Diego on the occasion of the apparitions over 450 years ago. We see a beautiful girl, perhaps fourteen years of age, with the olive skin and dark hair which characterized the Aztec people. Her rose-colored garment is overlaid with a lacy sheath adorned with a delicate design in gold. Her mantle is predominantly turquoise in color and is decorated with stars. She stands on the moon with an angel at her feet, eyes cast down and hands folded. The sun, hidden by her figure, sends out multiple rays all around her. She appears to be a maiden, a virgin, yet at the same time wears a maternity band about her waist, signifying that she is pregnant.

Each detail of the image carries a meaning which con-

Mary Ever-Virgin

tributed to acceptance of the Lady and, indeed, of Christianity, by the Aztecs. In the first place, the apparitions took place on the hill of Tepeyac, the site of a former pagan temple built in honor of Tonantzin, the Aztec virgin goddess, Mother of the Earth and Corn. Because she hides the sun but not its rays, the Indians understood that this Lady was more powerful than the sun-god Huitzilopochtli who filled them with fear and dread. Her foot rests in a position of victory, on the crescent moon, a symbol of Quetzalcoatl, the feathered serpent-god. The turquoise of the Lady's mantle was the color reserved for Aztec royalty. It was also the color which signified the great spirit, Omecihuatl, a god neither male nor female, who was thought of as the sole powerful creating force in the universe. Thus, she was a queen, but not a god, since her head was bent in humble submission and her hands were joined in the Indian gesture of offering. The colors of the image reflect the riches of nature so cherished by the Indians: tones of earth, sky and sea. She was one of them, and she spoke to Juan Diego not in Spanish, but in Nahuatl, the language of the Aztecs.

The Indians who looked at the image of the Virgin of Guadalupe found tenderness, compassion and goodness in the features of her face. They saw her as a mother preparing to give birth. Perhaps her child would be the one sent by their ancient gods to fulfill the prophecies which foretold the end of their civilization and the beginning of a new age of freedom and salvation. Liberation had not come, as many Indians had thought it would, with the Spanish Conquistadores. The Lady who looked and spoke like an Indian promised to bring them life, to make them a new people, to announce a new age.

Volumes have been written in an attempt to establish the authenticity of the story of Guadalupe and to belie the accusations of fraud by skeptics and enemies of religion. Most of the research has been centered on the more than four-centuries old image preserved on cloth that ordinarily carries a life-expectancy of some twenty years. The *tilma* of Juan Diego and the image it bears have endured the ravages of time, natural disaster and human malice. Still, there is no sign of decay in its texture or composition. Investigations by microscope, infra-red radiation and, more recently, computer-enhanced photography fail to explain in human terms the existence of the image. Extensive photographic experimentation has also been undertaken to demonstrate the amazing reflections of human faces in the cornea of each eye of the image—a phenomenon usual in the case of a photograph, but never of a painting.

In a similar way, studies have been undertaken to determine the nature of the "painting." The judgment of an eighteenth-century commission of artists who examined the image in detail was expressed in a statement that all four types of painting known at the time seemed to have been used: fresco, oil, water color and tempera. The physically impossible blending of these types on the rough surface of the *tilma* could not be explained. The complete absence

Mary Ever-Virgin

of brush strokes and the inability to ascertain the existence of whatever materials were used to produce the colors have also led, in other studies, to the conclusion that only a supernatural origin can explain this image of Mary. The extraordinary circumstances which have surrounded the image from the beginning are not more wonderful than the message entrusted to Juan Diego by the Virgin of Guadalupe.

THE MESSAGE

The words of Our Lady of Guadalupe have been recorded in what seems to be a sixteenth-century (c. 1573) account entitled, "Primitive Relation." This document was based on a previous text attributed to the man who translated Juan Diego's words into Spanish for the bishop to whom he was sent. A fuller written record which scholars date between 1551 and 1561 includes a simple, charming description of the events that took place on Tepeyac and in the bishop's palace, along with the conversations between the Lady and the Indian whom she addressed as "the most humble of my sons."

The message of Guadalupe can be considered on three different levels. At one level, we listen to the Lady's identification of herself. At another, we hear the mandate sent to Bishop Zumarraga. At a third, we discern the universal dimension of Mary's share in the mission of her son.

The young woman who appeared to Juan Diego identified herself as "the ever-virgin," "Holy Mary," "Mother of the True God," who is Creator of all things, Lord of heaven and earth. Mary also assured the Indian that she was his Mother, the "merciful Mother" of all who dwell on earth, of all who love her, invoke her and confide in her. Mary claimed to have many servants and messengers to whom she could entrust any of her wishes. She offered no explanation for her choice of Juan Diego, but insisted that he be the person to carry out this mission.

The Lady of Guadalupe wanted to be known as Virgin, as Mother of God and Mother of all people. She was Queen of those who were ready to serve her. She identified with the Indians of Mexico and brought with her the promise of life and hope for those who appealed to her for protection and assistance.

The Lady's message to Juan Diego was expressed in the form of a mandate. The first word of this mandate was a directive to the Indian to go to the bishop of Mexico City in her name. The second word was the communication of the Lady's desire that a "temple" or shrine be built on the hill of Tepeyac. The precise term she used to describe the temple is significant. The Virgin wanted a *teocalli*, a "house of God," a shrine where the true God was to be worshipped.

The message, at this level, becomes a call to the conversion of a whole people. The Spanish conquerors had not been able to bring about the Christianization of the Indians. This wonder was to be realized through a Spanish bishop, heeding the words of a poor peasant who spoke

Mary Ever-Virgin

in the name of the Virgin Mary. The succession of shrines constructed over the centuries—each church larger than the previous one—has borne witness to the devotion and the conversion of a people whose faith in Christ was the fruit of their devotion to his Mother. It is not an exaggeration to say that Mary "gave birth to the Mexican people" in giving birth to a renewed Christianity.

The phenomenon of a renewed Christianity introduces a universal dimension into the Virgin's message. The Lady who, almost playfully, addressed the Indian peasant as "Juanito" and "Juan Dieguito" was engaging in more than a casual exchange. She wanted him to understand that her love and concern enfolded him and reached beyond him: to his invalid uncle, to all the people of the land, to all who loved her everywhere. Juan's realization of the importance of her request inspired him to speak with simplicity and courtesy. "I am a nobody," he insisted and then flung out a torrent of words to describe himself: a "small rope," a "tiny ladder," the "tail end," a "leaf." Affectionately he could call her "my Child, the least of my daughters, my Lady." Together they were able to succeed and a work of worldwide consequence was initiated.

At first, the apparitions were known only in Mexico. Echoes of the events traveled quickly. Within thirty years after the happenings of Tepeyac, Pope Pius IV had a copy of the image in his private rooms and saw that models of Our Lady of Guadalupe were distributed. The victory at Lepanto, in 1571, was attributed to the protection of the Virgin of Guadalupe whose image had been placed in the

Christian flagship. Shrines and churches were built to honor Our Lady of Guadalupe in countries throughout the world. Decrees concerning her image have been issued by at least twenty-five popes since 1531, the year of the apparitions.

What does all this mean, except that the Virgin of Guadalupe proclaims a message that speaks to the heart of the entire Christian world, because it echoes the truth of the gospel preserved in the perennial teaching of the Church. In a unique way, Catholic doctrine concerning Mary's virginity is enhanced and illuminated by the image of Our Lady of Tepeyac.

THE TEACHING

Catholic teaching affirms Mary's divine maternity and her perpetual virginity as two most singular graces bestowed on her by God. The earliest recorded Christian prayer *(Sub tuum praesidium)* to Mary reflects these two mysteries:

> We fly to thy protection,
> O holy Mother of God.
> Do not reject the petitions
> We raise to you in our need,
> But deliver us always
> From all dangers,
> O glorious, blessed Virgin!

Mary Ever-Virgin

This third-century oration presents in a brief, poetic form the basic attitude toward Mary found in the early Christian community. Catholics have, historically, looked to both Scripture and Tradition to support their belief in Mary's virginity.

The Scriptural evidences for Catholic belief in the virginity of Mary have been the object of a great deal of study and discussion in recent years. Developments in New Testament exegesis have led to a "new" reading of the biblical texts. In particular, the infancy narratives have been analyzed according to a method of biblical criticism that takes historical, literary and cultural factors into account. This reading of the biblical texts often results in a "negative" witness, that is, in the absence of any denial of what the Church teaches. Furthermore, awareness of the intentions of the sacred writers in their proclamation of the gospel to a specific audience adds an important note in the analysis of any passage. Despite the absence of an explicit statement of Mary's perpetual virginity in the Scriptures, the faith of the Church has found a foundation for this doctrine in the Fathers of the early Church, in the teaching of Church Councils and in credal, liturgical and catechetical affirmations. As the American bishops wrote in their Pastoral Letter on the Blessed Virgin Mary (*Behold Your Mother: Woman of Faith*), Catholic belief in Mary's virginity is founded not on the Bible alone, but on the Bible as it has been read, interpreted and understood, under the guidance of the Holy Spirit, in the living Church.

Agnes Cunningham

The doctrine of Mary's virginity has always included three specific aspects: Mary's virginal conception of Christ; Mary's virginity in giving birth to Christ; Mary's virginity throughout her entire life, following Christ's birth. The phrases used to speak of these three aspects, respectively, are: *virginitas ante partum; virginitas in partu; virginitas post partum.*

In his letter to the Council of Chalcedon (A.D. 451), Pope Leo I clearly taught the doctrine of Mary's virginal conception of Christ. This teaching was the culmination of many earlier witnesses to the Church's belief that Jesus "was conceived of the Holy Spirit by the Virgin Mary." Early in the second century, St. Ignatius, bishop of Antioch in Syria, wrote to the Ephesians that the mysteries of Mary's virginity and child-bearing were hidden from "the Prince of this world." The greatest of the second-century Greek Apologists, Justin Martyr, understood that the prophet Isaiah (7:14) had foretold that the Christ would be "born through a virgin."

Irenaeus, the second-century bishop of the Church of Gaul, compared the "virgin Mary" to the "virgin Eve."

Tertullian included in his "rule of faith" an article that declared that the Word had entered the Virgin Mary "by the spirit and power of God" the Father. The "canon of truth" held by Irenaeus and Tertullian's "rule of faith" were both confirmed in the First Council of Constantinople (A.D. 381) in the creed now recited everywhere in the entire Catholic world during the eucharistic celebration on Sundays and major feasts throughout the year.

Mary Ever-Virgin

The question of Mary's virginity *in partu*, that is, while giving birth to Christ, raises an issue that is biological, more than it is theological. Some writers would argue that the denial of a truly "human" birth somehow lessened Christ's human nature and his share in the human condition, "like us in all things except sin." Also, the teaching of the Fathers, that Mary's bodily integrity was not violated in Christ's birth and that she was preserved from the ordinary pains of childbirth, seemed to make her more than human.

Throughout the fourth century, many of the great Fathers—bishops and theologians—taught Mary's virginity during the birth of Christ. Perhaps St. Augustine expressed it most clearly when he wrote, "She conceives and is a virgin; she gives birth and is a virgin." Like Augustine, the Latin Fathers affirmed Mary's bodily integrity *in partu*, while the Greek Fathers seemed to emphasize, rather, her freedom from pain in the joy of bringing Christ into the world. As Frederick M. Jelly, O.P., has pointed out in *Madonna*, Rahner's suggestion that Mary's human experiences were unique because she was totally free from all sin, is "most acceptable." It respects the delicate nature of the question under discussion, while providing doctrinal substance and meaning for Catholic faith.

When the Lady of Guadalupe identified herself to Juan Diego as the "Ever-Virgin," she was using an expression that had been a popular title for Mary from the second half of the fourth century and after. St. Epiphanius seems to have been the Church Father who was responsible for the insertion of this phrase into the Eastern Christian form of the Creed of Nicaea (A.D. 325). The title was seen as a way of counteracting the influence of heretics who took literally the scriptural reference to the "brothers" and "sisters" of Jesus in the New Testament. What else could this mean, but that Mary and Joseph had had other children? The teaching of Mary's virginity *post partum* was directly challenged by this interpretation of the biblical text.

The acceptance of Mary's perpetual virginity, including the preservation of her virginity following the birth of Jesus, became increasingly widespread. Frequently, affirmation of this teaching went hand-in-hand with references to Mary's divine maternity. In A.D. 553, the Second Council of Constantinople acknowledged these two doctrines. In A.D. 649, the Council of Lateran declared Mary's virginity to be perpetual. During the thirteenth century, the "divine and virginal motherhood of Mary" was included in the Fourth Lateran Council's "Profession of the Catholic Faith against the Albigensians and other Heretics."

Throughout the centuries, Catholic devotion to Mary has found expression in titles of affection and honor, many of them affirming her virginity. As early as the seventh or eighth century, she was saluted as "Holy Virgin of Virgins," in the Litany of the Saints, already widespread in Europe. The Litany of the Blessed Virgin (the Litany of Loreto) had been in use for several centuries, when it

Mary Ever-Virgin

was formally approved in 1587 by Pope Sixtus V. In this Marian prayer, Mary's virginity is hailed in ways that reflect some understanding of the dimensions of the mystery:

> Virgin most prudent,
> Virgin most venerable,
> Virgin most renowned,
> Virgin most powerful,
> Virgin most merciful,
> Virgin most faithful,
>   PRAY FOR US!

In a more recent adaptation of this litany, several new acclamations are included:

> Virgin Daughter of Zion,
> Virgin most pure and lowly,
> Virgin most meek and obedient.

The Litany of the Blessed Virgin Mary remains perennially popular. This fact is attested to, at one level, by the insertion or addition of titles given to Mary as a result of new theological or devotional understandings of her place in the Church. As we review the invocations that witness to love for Mary and to our desire to honor her, we pause at the words which proclaim her virgin. To what extent does this mystery speak to women and men today? How can our understanding of Mary's virginity help us in our efforts to share in the life and mission of the Church?

SIGNIFICANCE

The meaning of Mary's virginity in every age is rooted in what we can call the anthropological dimension of our life in Christ and the mission entrusted to him by the Father. In other words, that mystery by which the Word of God took flesh and was born of a virgin in view of our salvation casts light on the "mystery" of who we are to be as human beings.

This insight was first expressed in the second century of the Christian era by Irenaeus of Lyons who taught that it was necessary for one man "born of a virgin" to redeem through obedience what another man "fashioned out of virgin soil" had brought about through disobedience. Irenaeus saw that ADAM, that is, humanity, fashioned first from "virgin," that is, "untilled" earth, was restored to righteousness by the Word's birth from a virgin, Mary. In the fourth century, St. Anthanasius again compared Mary, virgin, to that "virgin soil" out of which God formed the first human being. We remember that "human" and "humility" both come from the Latin word for *soil (humus)*. We are reminded, once again, of the Virgin of Guadalupe and her identification with the poor, lowly Indians to whom she brought her Son's message of redemption.

Mary Ever-Virgin

Through Mary, virgin, our humanity has been ennobled and "divinized" through the grace of Christ, her Son.

In addition to an understanding of the fundamental reality of what we are as created and human, reflection on the contemporary significance of Mary's virginity can help us to appreciate what is meant by *integrity*. The physical aspect of this quality is readily understood, when we speak of virginity. In fact, the early Church Fathers are often accused of having contributed to a pessimistic view of sexuality by the way in which they promoted and extolled virginity, hence, bodily integrity.

Critics of the Fathers of the Church have failed to grasp the symbolic nature of physical integrity perceived by these early Christian writers. In their eyes, the virgin's integrity signified an inviolate commitment to Christ through faith and the affirmation of true doctrine. The virgin was one who witnessed to the integrity of unwavering faith in the Risen Lord as surely as the martyrs had done, when they surrendered their bodies to torture and death. The virgin was a sign in the Christian community of the "integrity," that is, adherence to the unsullied wholeness of the Church's doctrine, rather than to the false teachings and partial truths of heretics.

Mary's virginity encourages believers in every age to nourish and deepen the faith which is given to us in baptism. The virginity of the Mother of Jesus Christ challenges us to know and profess the "teaching which comes to us from the Apostles." In the mystery of Mary's virginity, we

Agnes Cunningham

find a new meaning of integrity, one that speaks to us as Christians and Catholics in today's world.

Finally, the virginity of Mary speaks to us of personal autonomy. Far from any notion of an individualistic self-centeredness, the psychological dimension of integrity points to a healthy independence and an interior unity which enable a human person to exercise responsible freedom in choices and decision making. Pope Paul VI highlighted these qualities of Mary's personality in his Apostolic Exhortation on renewal of devotion to the Mother of God, *Marialis cultus* (1974). In the biblical passages of the Lukan and Johannine gospel accounts, Mary is presented as a woman who is aware of her responsibilities and conscientious in fulfilling them. She does not hesitate to take initiative, where that is needed. She knows how to be present to every situation in a discreet and appropriate manner. The virginity of Mary becomes an inspiration and a model for personal growth in maturity, for women and men who seek to grow, also, to the fullness of the stature of Christ (cf. Eph. 4:13). In the process of that growth, our mentor and guide is Mary, Ever-Virgin, Mother of God.

The Ever-Virgin Lady who appeared to Juan Diego proclaimed a message of integrity for "all the Americas." Her presence was a prelude to the gift of faith in Jesus Christ, her Son. Conversion of the Mexican peoples led to knowledge of those teachings which call Christians in every age to resist error and the worship of idols. She inspired the Indian who was her messenger with courage and a sense

Mary Ever-Virgin

of inner conviction for the task entrusted to him. She brought assurance that the values of a rich, unique culture would be preserved in a people, threatened with exploitation and oppression, who were to find new life in Christ. The message of Guadalupe remains as eloquent today as it was nearly five centuries ago, at Tepeyac.

II. Mary: God-Bearing Mother

THE IMAGE

THE image of Mary as *THEOTOKOS* is one of the most cherished representations of Our Lady in the history of Christian devotion. In this image, we find Mary with the Child Jesus portrayed in a manner that appears strange to Western eyes. We are too accustomed to the realistic "holy cards," paintings and statues that look like the people we meet every day. The stylized lines of an *icon* strike us as "unreal," as "frozen" or distant. As a result, we frequently miss the rich artistry before us and fail to seize the message the icon has to communicate.

The image known as the *Theotokos* portrays the upper portion of Mary's body. She carries the child, seated upright on her left arm. As we look carefully at what seems, at first, to be a simple image, we begin to notice details which initially escaped our attention. The veil worn by Our Lady covers her head completely and falls in symmetrical folds around her face and shoulders like a cloak or mantle. The veil is rich in color, adorned with a jeweled border. On Mary's forehead and on each of her shoulders the artist has painted a star, although one is often hidden from view by the Child. Mary's gaze is turned toward us, while her right hand leads our eyes to the Child. Her face is serene, gentle and full of compassion.

The Child himself is small, with the face of an adult. His garments match those of his Mother, except that his cloak or mantle is of a brilliant color. In one hand he holds a book. The other hand is extended, with the index and middle fingers joined, apart from the others. The eyes of the Child are directed beyond the image at objects that are not always visible to us. His expression is serious, mature, royal. Behind the head of the Child and that of his Mother there is a golden halo. Inscriptions in Greek tell us that this is, indeed, the Mother of God *(MATER THEOU)* with the Child who is "the Alpha and the Omega, the First and the Last, the Beginning and the End" (Rev. 22:13).

Because this is one of the most ancient representations of Mary, we find variations of the basic portrayal described above. The paintings which show Mary pointing to the Child are known by the general title of the *Hodegetria*, "Pointer of the Way." Jesus *is* the Way; the *Hodegetria* carries a christological dimension. Another form of the *Theotokos* icon, the *Eleousa* style, portrays Mary holding the Child close to her. It emphasizes, rather, the motherhood of Mary. Icons painted in this style are frequently known as the Virgin of Compassion.

A number of legends have developed concerning the origin of the *Theotokos* icon. In 1887 the Christian historian, Ferdinand Gregorovius, recounted a legend until

Mary: God-Bearing Mother

then generally unknown. It seems that as St. Luke the Evangelist was approaching death, he admitted that he had carried with him for many years a genuine portrait of the Mother of Christ. He entrusted this portrait to his disciple, Ananias, for safekeeping after his death. Ananias took the icon from Thebes, where St. Luke died, to Athens. There, the painting was held in honor, under the title of the "Athenain" or the "Athea."

Some time later, during the reign of Theodosius the Great (A.D. 375-395), a Christian, Basilius Soterictus, was told in a dream to take the portrait to a safer place. Soterictus, accompanied by a band of pilgrims, traveled across land and sea to a mountain in what is now northeastern Turkey. There, near the city of Trebizond (Trabzon), they founded a monastery to which they gave the name Panagia. The word means, "All Holy," but, as informed authors have pointed out, in the Eastern Orthodox Church, the term has come to mean the Virgin Mary.

The legend continues, and we learn from a sixth-century chronicler that a beautiful painting of Mary was found in Jerusalem, in the fifth century. Allegedly, the portrait was discovered by Empress Athenais Eudokia, wife of Theodosius II. It was at that time that St. Luke was credited as having painted this portrait of Mary, as it was supposed that he had painted the portrait carried to the Panagia Monastery less than a century earlier. Were the two paintings one and the same? The legend neither affirms nor denies that suggestion.

Agnes Cunningham

The *Hodegetria*, we are told, was eventually (A.D. 538) installed in the great Church of Santa Sophia (Holy Wisdom), in Constantinople, after Empress Eudokia sent it to her sister-in-law, Saint Pulcheria. A letter written by Pope Innocent III on January 13, 1207, states that at the time of the Fourth Crusade, the portrait was moved for safekeeping to the Church of Christ Pantocrator. It is generally held that the *Hodegetria* was destroyed when the Turks conquered Constantinople in 1453.

Legends, however, die slowly. Robert de Clari, a thirteenth-century French historian, claims that the Greek emperors carried the icon known as *Hodegetria* whenever they went into battle. Another version of the story presents the claim that the painting was brought to Italy and placed in St. Mark's Basilica in Venice. Other stories are recounted from time to time. Some writers would claim that the *Hodegetria* was preserved at the time of the iconoclast controversy, in the eighth century, because it was hidden outside the city of Constantinople in a secret chapel. Again, the icon is supposed to have been taken from Santa Sophia in A.D. 988, when Princess Anna, the sister of Emperor Basil II, married Vladimir, Grand Duke of Russia.

Does the original *Hodegetria* still exist today? We shall consider the question once again, later in this chapter. For now, it is enough to recall that many opportunities existed for artists who might have wanted to copy the famous portrait. We ought not be surprised that this has been done. In fact, one of the most striking portrayals of *Theotokos* can be found in the splendid icon of Our Lady of Vladimir.

Mary: God-Bearing Mother

Because this icon represents many characteristics of twelfth-century Byzantine iconography, it merits our attention. In style, the icon of Our Lady of Vladimir combines both the *Hodegetria* and the *Eleousa* models. It seems to have been painted by a highly competent master of the iconographic method, shortly before 1131, when it was taken from Constantinople to Russia. In 1155, it was moved from Kiev to Vladimir, the city immortalized in the painting's title. Some time after 1395, it was transported to Moscow, where it continues to be regarded by those who can appreciate it as, perhaps, the nation's most sacred treasure. The icon of Our Lady of Vladimir is an outstanding example of why the art of iconography can be said to give us a "theology of beauty."

THE MESSAGE

In order to understand the meaning of the Church's teaching in calling Our Lady *"Theotokos,"* it is necessary to have some idea of the art style in which this image of Mary is presented. We have to try to understand what the icon is meant to be, if we want to hear the Word Mary brings to us; if we would see the Image Mary shows us.

The word, icon, comes from a Greek word *(EIKON)* which means *image*. The Jews of the Old Testament were forbidden, by law, to produce images, in order to preserve the purity of their worship of an invisible God, Yahweh. This prohibition was also a preparation for their acceptance of God's revelation in Christ, the Icon (Image) of God

35

Agnes Cunningham

par excellence. Indeed, as the Fathers of the Church tell us, when God created man *(HOMO)* in the beginning, it was "in the image" of God, that is, *in* the Word of God and *according to* the Image of God.

In A.D. 843, the Council of Constantinople definitively reaffirmed the veneration of icons, following the iconoclast crisis and the destruction of sacred images by those who rejected all representations of God, Christ, Mary and the saints. What the iconoclasts failed to grasp was the theological and spiritual reality which constituted the heart and the essence of the icon.

The elements of an icon are simple. They include the *sacred* (sacred time, sacred space) and the *beautiful*. Both of these elements exact from the iconographer the discipline of mind and spirit which leads to contemplation and the discipline of hand and eye which leads to the mastery of a difficult technique.

From the earliest ages of Christianity, the followers of Jesus knew how to engage in *visual* as well as in *verbal* theology. We in the West are more familiar with a theology that came to us in words. Words were spoken in catechetical instruction, in sacramental preparation or in liturgical celebration. Words were proclaimed in discourse, polemic or apologetic. Words were pastoral: in homilies and sermons; they were enlightening: through exegesis and reflection. The documents that come to us in the Scriptures and from the centuries of the patristic age (c. A.D. 95 - 608 [West]/A.D. 759 [East]) bear witness to the rich develop-

Mary: God-Bearing Mother

ment and significant contribution of a theology that was written to be read and spoken to be heard.

The visual transmission of the Good News of Jesus Christ also emerged early in the Christian experience. The walls of the rock-cave churches of Cappodocia, for example, are adorned with every story of the Old and New Testaments necessary for Christian instruction and adornments in catacombs, on sarcophagi, wherever Christians assembled. Christians were instructed, whether they were literate or illiterate. The tradition of Christian art was established. Iconography developed through three periods or ages, each one of which was marked by specific characteristics in the evolution of a "visual theology." The golden age of iconography occurred in the fourteenth century.

The person who aspires to be an iconographer must be willing to submit to the intense spiritual discipline that initiates one to the art of contemplation. The icon is a symbol of a mystery that is present, represented in and entered into through the icon. The icon is meant to touch the mind, the heart and the imagination with its message. It communicates an epiphany—a manifestation—of a presence that is transcendent. The iconographer must be able to contemplate the reality of the mystery he or she plans to represent. The iconographer must let the mystery inspire whatever representation will best transmit the meaning and message of the transcendent.

The second discipline to which the iconographer must submit is the discipline of the art. Icons are painted on wood, frequently, the wood of the cypress tree. A slightly depressed area is prepared, so that a natural frame is formed around the main area. A coat of adherant is spread so that canvas, covered by a layer of alabaster powder, can be fixed in place. As much as possible, the colors used by the artist must be taken from natural powders mixed with the yolk of an egg. When the painting is finished, a protective coat of the best linseed oil, mixed with various resins, is added. This furnishes a resistant, impenetrable finish which protects and preserves the original splendor of the colors.

Iconographic rules regarding the use of material, colors, lines or adornment are strictly indicated. The art of iconography is jealously guarded, passed on from a master to his disciples. Surprising as it may seem, no two icons—even those of the same subject, even in the same "school"—are ever identical. The discipline of the art is transformed by the discipline of contemplation. The result is a masterpiece that is solemnly blessed to become the focus-point for entrance into prayer and for personal contact with a heavenly presence and mystery.

Why this lengthy description of what seems to be a technical procedure: the painting of an icon? Quite simply, the painting of an icon is, actually, a spiritual experience both for the iconographer and for one who gazes on the finished products as well as a process which reflects an ever-deepening knowledge and veneration of the presence and the mystery into which we enter through prayerful reflec-

Mary: God-Bearing Mother

tion on the icon. In the case of the *Theotokos*, this is strikingly true.

St. John Damascene has said that the entire mystery of the economy of salvation is contained in the one word, *Theotokos*. We need time, as an iconographer does, to grasp the many dimensions of beauty revealed in the image of the God-bearing Mother. She is the new Eve, the figure of the new creation, yet she is one of us. In the words of the poet, Gerard Manley Hopkins, the icon of the *Theotokos*, like the Mother of God herself, has only one thing to do: "To let God's glory through." The luminous quality of the true icon is one of its most symbolic characteristics.

The icon of the *Theotokos* affirms the Church's ancient, never-changing belief that Mary is truly Mother of God. She is Mother of Jesus Christ, true God and true Man. She is Mother of the Child to whom she gave birth and Mother of the Body of Christ, the Church. The three stars on her forehead and shoulders proclaim her virginity before, during and after the birth of her child. The colors she wears declare that she is human with us, but exalted and royal, a true queen. The child is clothed in garments and colors that proclaim divinity and humanity. So too does the gesture of his right hand, with two fingers raised to signify the two natures that are his and the other three joined to affirm the Trinity of persons in God. The book he carries is the book of the Scriptures. In later representations of the *Theotokos*, the artist has shown us what the child sees:

Agnes Cunningham

the instruments of the Passion, held by ministering angels with veiled hands.

How does the icon of the *Theotokos* reflect the teaching of the Church concerning the divine maternity of Mary? What does the Church teach today about this privilege and mystery in the life of the Virgin of Nazareth? What is it that we affirm when we greet Mary as, *Theotokos!* or when we pray, as the entire Church does daily: *Holy Mary, Mother of God, pray for us!* To what extent does the *Theotokos* help us to understand what Vatican II meant by "the Blessed Virgin Mary in the mystery of Christ and of the Church"?

THE TEACHING

The word, *Theotokos*, seems to have been introduced into Christian theological vocabulary as early as Origen (+ c. A.D. 254) or Hippolytus (+ c. A.D. 236). It was used by the Greek Fathers as a title for Mary, the "God-bearer." The title was defended by Bishop Alexandria of Antioch (+ A.D. 328) and became, in time, a term of devotion.

In the year A.D. 429, use of the word was questioned by Nestorius (+ c. 451), bishop of Constantinople, who objected to giving the title to a human being. Nestorius claimed that a more appropriate way of speaking about Mary would be to call her *"Christotokos,"* the Christ-bearer. Nestorius was concerned about preserving the integrity and completeness of the humanity of Christ. He

Mary: God-Bearing Mother

also found it impossible to acknowledge that a human being could give birth to God. *Theotokos,* he claimed, gave the impression that Mary was a goddess who has begotten divinity.

St. Cyril of Alexandria (+ A.D. 444) was the theologian who challenged Nestorius and his teaching. As the debate progressed through correspondence between the two bishops, it became clear that the controversy was not going to be easily or quickly resolved. The fourth ecumenical council of the Church was convoked at Ephesus in A.D. 431 to address what was perceived as a serious doctrinal and theological problem. The decisions of the Council were important for later teaching on Christ as well as on Mary. Nestorius was condemned, and Cyril's Second Letter to Nestorius was cited as an expression of orthodox Catholic faith: "Thus [the Holy Fathers of the Church] have not hesitated to call the holy Virgin Theotokos." With this teaching, the Fathers of the Council affirmed that Christ was true God as well as true man, from the first moment of the Incarnation.

Nestorius had been disturbed by what is called the "communication of idioms." The meaning of this phrase is that, because of the mystery of the hypostatic union, anything that can be properly and concretely affirmed of Christ's manhood can also be attributed to God. For example, we can say that Jesus Christ was born of the Virgin Mary; therefore, it can be said that God was born of the Virgin Mary. When we call Mary, *Theotokos,* we profess that her

41

son existed as one divine person in whom the two natures of divinity and humanity are perfectly united.

The word, *Theotokos*, had been in use in theological and devotional language for at least one hundred years before it was given official—that is, canonical—status at the Council of Ephesus. It might be objected that the conciliar teaching was, actually, a departure from the evidences of the New Testament. St. Thomas Aquinas addresses this objection by pointing to the biblical teaching that Christ is God and to the fact that the Scriptures tell us that Mary is his mother. In other words, the development of doctrine that took place in the Christian community, over several centuries, was rooted in the biblical teaching. The doctrine of the Council, as Aquinas notes, is a specific, precisely stated teaching. Mary is Mother of Christ, who is God; she is not the Mother of either God the Father or God the Holy Spirit. She is not the Mother of divinity.

The Church's teaching that Mary is *Theotokos* has been affirmed throughout the centuries. The *Leonine Sacramentary*, generally attributed to Pope Leo I (+ A.D. 461) contains an addition to the Canon of the Mass (the Eucharistic Prayer) which refers to "the glorious ever-Virgin Mary, Mother of God" *(Theotokos)*. In the Christological definition of the Council of Chalcedon (A.D. 451), Mary was again called *Theotokos*, Mother of God. In the year 534, Pope John II declared in a letter that Mary is "truly the Mother of God." Ten years later, the Second Council of Constantinople restated the teaching of the Divine Mater-

Mary: God-Bearing Mother

nity of Mary, as did the Third Council of Constantinople (A.D. 680-81).

In spite of the fact that Mary has been acknowledged and honored as Mother of God in the entire Catholic world, the title *Theotokos* has not been familiar in the West until recently. A good part of the reason for this may be that the word itself is Greek and that translation into English of its rich significance is difficult. While we can certainly say that *Theotokos* means Mother of God or God-bearer, we can also try to capture something of the original signification in terms like: "Birth-Giver of God," the "God-bearing Mother," the "Bringer-forth-of-God." Devotion to Mary, Mother of God, in the West has been reflected in and nurtured by titles such as those found in the Litany of Loreto:

> Holy mother of God, . . .
> Mother of Christ, . . .
> Mother of divine grace, . . .
> Mother of our Creator,
> Mother of our Savior.

It is primarily in the Eastern Christian tradition that this ancient title for Mary has been preserved. In the Divine Liturgy of the Byzantine Church, for example, the word, *Theotokos*, is so frequently proclaimed that even ears unaccustomed to a sacred language other than English (or Latin) can recognize it. The separated Churches of the

43

East, also, treasure this title for Mary. The word, *Theotokos,* is truly one of the most "catholic" (universal) ways in which Christians can address the Mother of God.

One of the most recent affirmations of Mary as Mother of God occurred in the Dogmatic Constitution on the Church, *Lumen gentium,* promulgated during the Second Vatican Council (November 21, 1964). A separate chapter on Mary had not been prepared in the original *schema* on the Church at Vatican II. Chapter VIII is the section of the document that presents Catholic teaching on the "glorious ever Virgin Mary, Mother of God and of our Lord Jesus Christ," as the text of the Canon of the Roman Mass refers to her. Throughout the chapter, Mary is repeatedly given titles that recall *Theotokos.* She is truly the Mother of God; Mother of the Son of God; Mother of the Redeemer; Mother of Our Lord and Savior. The entire chapter is a reflection of Mary and her place in the mystery of Christ and of the Church. Developments in Mariology in the last twenty years have taken *Lumen gentium,* chapter VIII as a point of departure for deepened theological research on Mary and renewal of authentic Catholic devotion to her.

SIGNIFICANCE

On May 16, 1975, Pope Paul VI addressed the International Mariological and Marian Congresses meeting in Rome, on renewal of devotion to Mary. The Pope's remarks

Mary: God-Bearing Mother

on that occasion lead us to reflect, once again, on the image of Mary as *Theotokos*. They call us to contemplate the Mother of God in this ancient portrayal of the mystery into which she has been summoned by God. Paul VI began by affirming the need to encourage renewal of devotion to Mary through the "way of truth," that is, through "biblical, historical and theological study of Mary's proper place in the mystery of Christ and the Church." He then exhorted his hearers to explore another way: the "way of beauty."

The "way of beauty" is a path that is opened to us through the medium of iconography. Contemplation on the icon of the *Theotokos* is contemplation of Mary in the beauty with which God has gifted and graced her in the mystery of her divine maternity. Here we recognize one aspect of the meaning the Mother of God, portrayed as *Theotokos,* can have for us. The "way of truth" and the "way of beauty" taken together represent the best theological traditions of both Eastern and Western Christianity. In the West, Christ has been primarily represented as the Word *(LOGOS)* of God; in the East, Christ has been thought of, rather, as the Image *(EIKON)* of God. Word and Image together transmit a richer concept of the mystery of Christ than either one or the other considered in itself. In terms of the reality of Church, it is clear that the wealth of Christianity, from the earliest ages, was to be found in the diversity which marked the true Apostolic Tradition in the local churches of the East and of the West.

Agnes Cunningham

From still another point of view, "truth" and "beauty" can be understood to refer to developments in theological methodology and reflection. Many people today—and, in a specific way, women—search for a theology that incorporates experience as well as intellect. Pastoral, spiritual and "story" theologies, for reasons which differ from one to the other, are considered to provide this more "balanced" approach. In fact, all theological methods would be enhanced by attention to the dimension of *beauty* as well as to that of *truth*.

These considerations help us to discern in this approach to Catholic veneration of Mary an unexpected ecumenical possibility. We have already realized that the *Theotokos* is an image that draws together both Eastern and Western Catholics, both Catholics and Orthodox Christians. The christological character of the Marian doctrine of the *Theotokos* can be of help to non-Catholic Christians who seek sincerely to understand the place given to Mary in Catholic teaching. When the mystery of Mary's motherhood is presented with its rightful emphasis on the mysteries of the Incarnation and Redemption in the life of her son, many misunderstandings and difficulties can be dispelled.

Another area of significance for us in the Motherhood of Mary is related, again, to the icon of the *Theotokos,* specifically, to the *Hodegetria*. Earlier in this chapter, in reviewing the legends that have surrounded the sacred image, one question was left unanswered: Is it possible that the original portrait of Mary still exists today? The ques-

tion is not facetious, but is founded on certain similarities
detected between the *Hodegetria Theotokos* and, perhaps,
two other images of Mary: Our Lady of Czestochowa and
the Virgin of Guadalupe. The similarity is found in what
is known as the tradition of the "Black Madonna."

The tradition of the Black Madonna can be traced to
a mid-fourth century monk who, it seems, discovered three
statues of the Virgin Mary. According to legend, the statues
were given to churches in Sardinia and Italy. It would seem
that one of them still exists and can be seen in the San-
tuario d' Oropa, to the northeast of Turin. This statue,
about three feet in height, is made of cedarwood; it portrays the Mother who carries the child, as she raises her
arms in prayer. The Madonna is called, "Black," because
of the dark color of Mary's complexion. This is the
characteristic which links every portrayal of Mary included
in the Black Madonna tradition. It is one of the details
which suggest that the original portrait attributed to St.
Luke may, in fact, have been brought to Poland in 1382
by a Ukranian Prince, Ladislaus Opolszyk, where it is kept
to this day.

The dark skin of Our Lady of Czestochowa, the olive
complexion of the Virgin of Guadalupe, and the "brown-
ish, or . . . chestnut color" of the "Lukan" portrait as it has
been described by a fourteenth-century Byzantine historian, seem to reflect an ancient tradition of dark-colored,
Greek Madonnas which were considered to be miraculous.
The Virgin of Guadalupe, particularly, is known as *"La*

Agnes Cunningham

Morena," the "dark-complexioned woman." The *Vierge Noire* ("Black Virgin") honored throughout France in medieval times also belongs to this tradition. Shrines can still be found in France and Spain where the Black Madonna or Virgin is revered.

This may sound highly interesting, but much of it is conjecture and seems not to cast any light on the meaning of Catholic teaching that Mary is *Theotokos,* Mother of God. However, another argument can be stated. In the first place, the striking similarities of artistic details in the icon-type images of Mary seem to attest to an oral tradition that can be traced to the earliest days of Christianity. The portrayal of Mary as a woman who can be quite readily identified as a Jewish maiden or mother, because of the color of her skin, speaks to us of the cultural reality in the midst of which she and her son lived.

Furthermore, the Black Madonna has earned her title in still other ways. At times, her complexion is dark because of the pigment in the colors used by the artist. At other times, however, the darkened complexion is the result of candles offered by pilgrims to a shrine or by devout believers who choose to honor the son by honoring his Mother. There have been moments in history, too, when the Black Madonna became the consoler and support of a people caught in a dark moment of struggle or oppression. The Black Madonna seems to have taken into her arms, with her son, the burdens and cares of a people. In later portrayals of the *Theotokos* icon, this fact is borne out, as was

Mary: God-Bearing Mother

noted earlier, by the presence in the portrait of angels displaying the instruments of Christ's future passion. Mary, *Theotokos*, God-bearing Mother, Black Madonna, is truly, as Pope John Paul II wrote in his encyclical, *Redemptoris Mater* ("The Mother of the Redeemer"), "the spiritual mother of humanity." Mary, *Theotokos*, is the *eschatological icon of the Church*, as Christians have hailed her through the ages. Mary, *Theotokos*, as St. John Eudes perceived, is that resplendent icon through which the glory of Christ shines upon us to enlighten and confirm our faith and our love.

III. Mother of the Church

THE IMAGE

ONE of my favorite representations of Mary is a statue in the Lady Chapel, of the Metropolitan Cathedral of Christ the King in Liverpool, England. The cathedral itself, consecrated on Pentecost Sunday, May 14, 1967, is contemporary in style, the work of Sir Frederick Gibberd, architect of London Airport. The Lady Chapel is one of twelve chapels designed for devotion as well as for providing solid areas between the buttresses of the cathedral. The "Lady Statue" is situated on a high ledge, at the point where two walls meet at the rear of the chapel. The statue is of terracotta. The artist was Robert Brumby. Each time I have visited the Liverpool Roman Catholic Cathedral, I have found this to be a truly remarkable statue.

The statue represents Mary standing behind a small child who could be about eight or nine years of age. Both Mother and child are barefoot, simply and similarly clothed. His arms are outstretched and uplifted, it would seem in excitement. His eyes are open wide and an expresison of interest and enthusiasm is on his face. He looks as if he is ready to run off toward something or someone. One is surprised, in looking at him a second time, to see that he has not moved.

Mary stands behind her son. She is at least twice as tall as he is, so that even though she is standing upright, one has the impression of a slight inclination of her body toward the child. It is at this point that one notices her arms. They are extremely long, almost too long for her body. She reaches out, so that the palms of her hands support the child's fingers. It is difficult to say whether the Mother is trying to push the child forward or hold him back. Her expression does not tell us, either. She, too, seems to be looking ahead, wide-eyed and serious, but at peace. She seems to be trying to discern the child's readiness for whatever lies ahead. She does not intend to let him go before he is ready; she has no intention—although she may have an intense desire—to hold him back, once he is prepared.

The Lady Statue in the Liverpool Cathedral represents two quite different perspectives. On the one hand, the artist has sought to portray a Mother and child who reflect new developments in religious devotional art. One wants to stand straight and tall in the presence of this Mary and Jesus. One wants to pray for clear-sightedness to discern one's path, for strength and readiness to embrace whatever lies ahead.

On the other hand, the artist has simply given us another statue of the Mother and her Child. It is true that we do not often see Jesus portrayed at the age of eight or nine. That is a novel touch. However, as we have seen already

Mother of the Church

in this book, the earliest Christian understanding of Mary was influenced by her relationship to her son, Jesus Christ. Devotion to Mary, from the earliest years of the Christian era, was christological in nature. With the beginnings of Christian art, the Mother was rarely portrayed without the son.

This association of Mary with Jesus was depicted in artistry and expressed in teaching. Early references to Mary outside the New Testament can be found as early as the beginning of the second century of the Christian Era. St. Justin, a philosopher and martyr, for example, speaks of Mary as the "second Eve," because of her association with Christ, the "second Adam." This theme was developed by Irenaeus, the second-century bishop of the church in Gaul.

As Fathers and theologians prepared for the Council of Ephesus (A.D. 431), they consulted the Scriptures to determine the degree to which Mary had been present with her son. They found her when the mystery of the Incarnation was announced. She was present at the birth of Jesus, during his childhood and at key moments during the years of his public ministry. They recognized her at the foot of the Cross and realized that was the occasion when she became Mother of the Whole Christ, symbolized in John. They understood that her presence in the Upper Room at the first Pentecost confirmed her as Mother of the Church, still in its infancy.

As Christian art developed through the centuries, painters and sculptors vied with one another to portray Mary and Christ in representations that could capture our attention and inspire our devotion. One of the most unique of these is a masterpiece which is in the Louvre, in Paris. The artist entitled this work, "Our Lady, Mediatrix of Grace," although it represents Mary as Mother of the Church, the Body of Christ. She stands, appearing larger than life, within the arches of a magnificent basilica. Her robe is ornate; her mantle, voluminous. She extends it on either side to enfold a multitude of people: kings and queens; bishops, monks and nuns; soldiers and scholars; saints and sinners. Pressing close to Mary, like little children, they all look to her with trust and confidence. One almost hears their petition: *After this, our earthly exile is ended, show us thy womb's most precious fruit, Jesus!*

The understanding that any representation of Mary and her son is symbolic of Mary and the Church is not particularly widespread. The painting in the Louvre is, obviously, more graphic. Nonetheless, certain statues or images seem to lend themselves more readily to the interpretation expressed in the words of a thirteenth-century English Cistercian who stated that Mary is understood to be Mother of the Body, since she is surely Mother of the Head. A further reflection on the Lady Statue in the Liverpool Cathedral will demonstrate this point.

THE MESSAGE

Perhaps, the most eloquent detail of the statue in the Lady Chapel of the Liverpool Cathedral is found in the

Mother of the Church

hands of the Mother and Child. At any moment, or so it seems, she can fold her fingers around his, to hold him back, or she can impel him forward with the force of her palms. Although everything else in the posture of the bodies and the barefoot feet of the Mother and Child seems settled or "planted" where they are, the energy focused by the artist in the two pairs of hands invests the woman and her son with vitality and movement.

A number of impressions are communicated by the image. The strongest of these is the sense of *mission*. The child is eager to run forward, to embrace or take hold of something in his line of vision. The Mother has to decide if it is good for him to go: is he ready? is he sufficiently prepared? The question does not seem to be whether or not he ought to go; it is, rather, when shall he go? The Mother is thus called on to discern well, to decide with wisdom. She has to weigh the benefits possible for her child, along with the good to be effected "out there."

The Lady Statue also impresses one as an artistic representation that demonstrates the decision to incoporate into an image of Mary characteristics that are a departure from the way she is usually portrayed. Here is a woman who is strong, determined, ready for action and decision making. She is attractive, but not at all "pretty" in the way many statues of Mary are. She is clearly "in charge" and capable of being so. Still, she is not harsh or unfeeling. She is at peace within herself and so she has a heart of compassion for others.

Agnes Cunningham

There is something about the Lady Statue that recalls the gospel account of the wedding feast at Cana (Jn. 2:1-11). Mary and Jesus were present there, guests at a joyful celebration. The evangelist portrays Mary as a woman whose sensitivity and awareness of a situation alerted her to an impending problem. With more than "womanly intuition," she recognized the "signs" of the moment and knew what action had to be taken. Her action was to speak to Jesus, visiting with his disciples and the other guests. Like the Mother in the Lady Chapel, she stood behind him, symbolically, and thrust him forward with the spiritual energy that was hers. Her words to the waiters were simple, full of confidence and certitude: "Do whatever he tells you." Despite the answer Jesus had given his Mother, distancing himself from her concern, he, too, chose to act: "Jesus performed this first of his signs at Cana in Galilee."

Another association brought to mind by the statue in the Lady Chapel is the description of Mary given by Pope Paul VI in the Apostolic Exhortation, *Marialis cultus*, on renewal of devotion to the Blessed Virgin Mary. In sections 34-37, Paul VI urges us to take a "new look" at Mary, in the light of the findings of the human sciences. From that perspective, we find that Mary can, indeed, be looked to as a model for contemporary women and men in the home, in politics, in social and cultural activities. Mary was capable, Pope Paul VI points out, of a "courageous choice" in her response to God's call. She was "far from being a timidly submissive woman or one whose piety was

Mother of the Church

repellent to others." Rather, she affirmed without hesitation God's vindication of the lowly and the oppressed. Mary knew poverty, suffering, flight and exile. She was, in every situation, a "woman of strength."

A composite emerges from statues like that of Mary and the Christ Child in the Lady Chapel, when taken with the story of Cana and the image portrayed by Pope Paul VI. Here is a woman truly called to be MOTHER in a uniquely particular way as well as in an extraordinarily universal manner. When speaking of Mary, the title, "Mother of the Church," resonates as a corollary to that of "Mother of God." Indeed, both history and tradition bear witness to the fact that Mary can rightly be addressed as "Mother of the Church," "Mother of the Mystical Body," "Mother of the Whole Christ-Head and Members."

A formal proclamation of Mary as "Mother of the Church" was made by Pope Paul VI on November 21, 1964, in his closing address to the third session of the Second Vatican Council. In his statement, the Pope spoke in terms that emphasized the rich dimensions of Mary's universal and spiritual maternity. His words bring us back, once again, to the Lady Statue and to the sense of *mission* she seems to communicate. It could readily be said that the Mother, with and through her child, expresses concern for all who would be committed to a Church-in-mission. Mary has frequently been called Christ's first disciple. She might also be saluted as the first Christian missionary. Certainly, the story of Cana would support that claim. Her care for "all the faithful and the pastors" of the Church, as Pope Paul insisted in this proclamation, lends more support to the argument.

The idea of Mary as "missionary" or "apostolic" is not entirely new. In the nineteenth century, Venerable Francis Mary-Paul Libermann, a convert from Judaism, founded the Society of the Holy Heart of Mary for missionary work, especially in Africa. This group was later joined, under Libermann's leadership, with an older congregation (Congregation of the Holy Ghost); the new religious family became known as the Spiritans. Building on the teaching of St. John Eudes (1601-1680), Father, Doctor and Apostle of the Heart of Mary, Libermann developed his understanding of the "eminently apostolic" heart of Mary. He looked to Mary as the model and source of every apostolate. Mary has given us an example of thirst for the coming of the reign of God. She inspires us to work for the proclamation of the gospel throughout the world.

The idea of Mary as an "apostle" in Libermann's sense should not sound strange to our ears. If we have reflected seriously on the image of the Mother and the Child in the Lady Chapel, we must know that her care is for the whole Christ. The Mother of God is truly Mother of the Church. Catholic teaching through the centuries has proclaimed and reaffirmed this truth.

THE TEACHING

When Pope Paul VI formally proclaimed Mary "Mother of the Church" at the conclusion of the third session of the

Mother of the Church

Second Vatican Council, he spoke for the Church-at-large and expressed a truth which had long been held by Catholics. In tracing the history of this title, however, it is difficult to identify specific texts or documents that clearly call attention to it. In searching the Scriptures, biblical scholars claim that texts in the first two chapters of Luke and passages in the gospel according to John support the concept.

St. Augustine is cited as the earliest authority from the patristic era who speaks of Mary as Mother of the members of Christ's body, as she is Mother of the Head. Further development of the idea can be found throughout the Middle Ages. The title, "Mother of the Church," was used for the first time in the twelfth century. A nineteenth-century theologian, Joachim Ventura (1792-1861), provided a theological foundation for understanding Mary's "ministry" as Mother of the Church, through his interpretation of John 19:26-27: "Woman, there is your son.". . . "There is your mother." It was also in the nineteenth century that the first serious work, using the title as its own, was published.

Pope Paul VI was not the first Pope to refer to Mary as "Mother of the Church." Benedict XIV, Leo XIII, Pius X, Pius XII and John XXIII all used the title. Leo XIII wrote of her as "Mother of the Church, the teacher and Queen of the Apostles." On February 2, 1904, St. Pius X promulgated the encyclical, *Ad diem illum*, linking Mary's spiritual motherhood to the mystery of the Incarnation.

It has been pointed out by more than one writer that Pope Paul's proclamation of Mary as "Mother of the

Agnes Cunningham

Church" provided a solution to one of the problems that arose during the Second Vatican Council. A number of the Council Fathers and *periti* had hoped for a separate document on Mary. Other Fathers and theological consultants were convinced that such a move would be undesirable biblically, ecclesiologically and ecumenically. Inclusion of the *schema* on Mary as the final chapter in the Dogmatic Constitution on the Church *(Lumen gentium)* was decided by a narrow margin (1114 to 1074 votes). The contents of the chapter were to present classic Catholic teachings in the area of Mariology, although there had been many petitions that a new doctrine—that of her role as "Mediatrix of All Grace"—be proclaimed.

Opposition to the Marian *schema* seems to have been based on the title first proposed for chapter VIII: Mary, Mother of the Church. Following debate, interventions and discussion, the theological commission decided against the use of the title. However, the direct appeal of several hundred Fathers to Pope Paul VI led to his decision in favor of the title in the proclamation made at the conclusion of the third session of the Council.

Closely related, historically, to the title, "Mother of the Church," is another: Mother of Divine Grace. This way of referring to Mary is an acknowledgment of her *spiritual motherhood*. Historically, this concept has been understood as another way of affirming that the Mother of God is our mother, also. The scriptural basis for this idea is the same as that used to support the teaching that Mary is Mother

60

Mother of the Church

of the Church: John 19:25-27. Scripture scholars will include John 1:12-13, John 16:21, Romans 2:19 and Revelation 12, when taken together, as significant texts as well. A concise statement of the explanation is simply that, when Mary became the Mother of our Savior in the physical order, she became our Mother in the order of grace.

The patristic evidence for Mary's spiritual motherhood is not explicit and where it exists, it is neither specific nor abundant. Nevertheless, a cumulative teaching can be traced from the Church Fathers, from Irenaeus through Augustine. An eighth-century Benedictine, Ambrose Autpert (+ A.D. 784), provided the earliest theological argument in support of Mary's spiritual motherhood: "How should she not be the Mother of the elect, she who gave birth to their brother?... why should she who brought forth Christ not be the Mother of believers?"

The spiritual motherhood of Mary has been taught by the Popes, beginning with Leo XIII, as another aspect of her universal motherhood. For Pope Paul VI, it was another way of expressing that Mary is Mother of the Church. A careful reading of *Lumen gentium*, chapter VIII, leads to an awareness that the central theme of that chapter is Mary's spiritual motherhood. The beginning of this maternity is identified with her "Yes," to the angel at the Annunciation and was confirmed on Calvary. It "will last without interruption until the eternal fulfillment of all the elect...."

Since the close of Vatican II, Mariologists have continued

to explore the Marian themes which emerged during the Council. In particular, they have studied the relation between Mary and the Church, since she is hailed as member, model and Mother of the Church. They have also sought to undertake research on Mary and the Holy Spirit, through whom she conceived Jesus Christ, our Lord and Savior. A revival and renewal of devotion to Mary in the last several years can be attributed, in great part, to the efforts of theologians and biblical scholars who have attempted to clarify and develop the rich insights of the Fathers of the Second Vatican Council as they reflected on Mary.

SIGNIFICANCE

Renewal and increase of devotion to Mary did not take place immediately after Vatican II. Developments in biblical studies and liturgical renewal seemed to call for a readjustment in the devotional life of Catholics and the modification of what had seemed to be exaggerations of personal piety in the Church. Demytholgization was adopted as a principle and a criterion in this process. Emergence of the Charismatic movement in the United States focused attention on the Holy Spirit—once called "the forgotten Person of the Trinity." Pneumatology was the latest title in a range of "new" theologies.

It must be recognized that the life of the Church-at-large and the spiritual lives of individual Church members have been enriched immeasurably by these developments. It was time for a renewal of biblical studies in the Catholic Church and for a renewed appreciation of and familiarity with the written Word of God. The liturgy had to be restored as the summit and source of all the Church's activity. As a spirit and grace of renewal were poured out in a "new Pentecost" upon the faithful, diverse methods and experiences of prayer became important—even, necessary. Serious theological studies on the Holy Spirit have been produced to enlarge and enlighten our understanding of the One God who is Three in Person.

In the United States, other influences militated against renewal of devotion to Mary and acceptance of her as "Mother of the Church." One of these factors was the Women's Liberation Movement and with it, the rise of "Christian Feminism." The Liberation Movement in all its phases called for the rejection, in religious questions, of any suggestion of oppression or subjection of peoples. The seeds of a new nationalism, sown in the United States through these movements was to bring about a rejection of "tradition" in the Roman Catholic Church and a strong orientation toward a future shaped by the new People of God.

Pope Paul VI was committed to the renewal of Marian devotion which had been perceived as necessary, even before Vatican II. In February, 1974, he promulgated the Apostolic Exhortation for the right ordering and development of the cult of the Blessed Virgin Mary. In 1975, he

Agnes Cunningham

addressed a letter on the same theme to participants of the Marian Congress meeting in Rome.

If we try to understand the resistance to Mary that has come from women, it is necessary to examine, at least briefly, some arguments affirmed by feminist writers. One of the first objections to any "exaltation" of Mary is based on the fact that she is already unique and held in veneration above all other members of her sex. Honor given to Mary as alone worthy to bear the son of God makes of every other woman, it is maintained, a "second-class citizen." Only one woman could be Mary. The rest are "daughters of Eve." Some feminists have been quick to blame Mary for the discrimination and oppression experienced by other women in a patriarchal Church.

The teaching that Mary is not only Mother of God, but also Mother of the Church is especially unacceptable to feminists. The uniqueness of her person is unduly highlighted, they would claim, by a "unique" motherhood that is divine, spiritual and universal. The concept of *motherhood* as a way of life and an ideal for women is based on the perception of woman as a "functional" being; one who exists for the service and pleasure of men; one who must be subject to her husband; one whose value consists in the fact that she can be reduced to a "sex object"; one whose importance lies in what her body can do and produce.

Added to these perceptions, the ways in which Mary has been portrayed in art and devotional literature, especially since the nineteenth century, have been distasteful to

Mother of the Church

feminists. They reject the image of a submissive, docile maiden, preserved from sin, cast in blue-and-white "perfection." Who can relate to such a person? feminists ask. Women need a real "flesh-and-blood" role-model to survive in a male-dominated world!

The teaching of Pope Paul VI on Mary's divine, spiritual and universal motherhood addresses such concerns as those expressed above. In complete fidelity to the biblical evidences, to the Apostolic Tradition and to the constant voice of the Church, Pope Paul VI presents a picture of Mary that is compatible with the highest aspirations of contemporary men and women. In a most particular manner, the image of Mary described by the Pope portrays an example of the faith and discipleship to which the entire Church and all members of the Church are called.

In her motherhood, Mary is the woman of faith par excellence. In her care and concern for the whole Christ, she shows forth the characteristics of a true disciple of the Lord. In a strange kind of paradox, Mary is Mother of the Church and Mother of Divine Grace because she is, first of all, a member of the Church. Her spiritual motherhood reflects the grace and virtue which are hers as one who believed in and followed Jesus in a pre-eminent manner.

Devotion to Mary has, indeed, been revitalized and renewed. For one thing, there has been a widespread resurgence of popular religion. The great Marian shrines have once again become centers of prayer and devotion. Alleged apparitions of Mary in several countries of Europe, Africa and South America in recent years have provoked curiosity as well as piety. The challenge remains to continue to promote the "right ordering" of devotion to Mary and to avoid what Michael O'Carroll calls " the extremes of naive credulity and irreverent scepticism."

It is advisable, too, to remind ourselves that "imitation is the highest expression of devotion." Throughout the ages, Mary as Mother has been the inspiration, the comforter and the model of generations of Christian mothers. As Mother of Jesus Christ, she exemplified the care, love and nurturing that provide the necessary atmosphere in which children and youth develop and grow to healthy adulthood. As Mother of the Church, Mary exercised a spiritual motherhood that has led generations of devoted, unmarried women—lay and religious—to cherish and serve the neglected, the abandoned, the forsaken; to assure spiritual and human formation to those who would otherwise be deprived of love, compassion and friendship.

Recent writings by thoughtful feminist authors, too, have begun to reflect the insight that the manner in which Mary exercised her Motherhood—whether divine, spiritual or universal—reveals a woman worthy of acclaim. She is a woman whose motherhood has enhanced those qualities of personhood which enables her to stand shoulder-to-shoulder with any woman who aspires to stature, participation in decision making and responsible action for the good of humankind.

IV. Mary, Mother of Sorrows

THE IMAGE

THE title, "Mother of Sorrows," ordinarily brings to mind an image of Mary standing at the foot of the Cross on Calvary. Catholic devotion has inspired artists, hymnodists and poets to portray her in just that posture. Every year, during the Lenten season, one refrain, in particular, rises from Churches and chapels:

> *Stabat Mater dolorosa*
> *juxta crucem lacrymosa*
> *dum pendebat filius.*

The popular translation is less graphic:

> At the Cross her Station keeping
> Stood the mournful Mother weeping
> Close to Jesus to the last.

The image of Mary standing at the foot of the Cross on Calvary, however, is not the representation we are going to consider in this chapter. Rather, I suggest that we turn our attention to another image: the Pieta. This image

67

presents Mary, either alone or with other gospel figures, usually John the Evangelist and Mary Magdalene, just after the body of Christ has been taken down from the cross. The Mother is in grief, mourning the dead son whom she holds on her knees.

The Pieta seems to have emerged as both a literary and an artistic theme in the Middle Ages, as efforts were made to portray the Virgin's sorrow during the period from the crucifixion to the burial of Jesus. The poems and sermons of the mystics reflect this theme, and it is not uncommon for an association to be made between the Pieta and the desolate mothers of the slaughtered Holy Innocents.

The earliest Pieta as we have come to know it, with Mother and son alone, is usually attributed to German artists of the early fourteenth century. During the fourteenth and fifteenth centuries, the image of the "St. Mary Elegy" or, the Pieta, as Italian artists called it, was developed. It is possible to distinguish several stages in the evolution of this image of the *Mater dolorosa*. The earliest German type shows Christ in a sitting position. The Italian style presents Christ across the Virgin's knees, his body in horizontal position. In France, the body of Christ is almost vertical, like a curve, sloping against the body of Mary.

Michelangelo, who is best known for this image because of the extraordinary Vatican Pieta, is the artist whose work will concern us here. He actually produced four Pietas, the earliest of which (1498) is in St. Peter's Basilica in Rome. As moving as each of the sculptured pieces is, the

Mary, Mother of Sorrows

statue of Mother and Son which speaks, perhaps, most eloquently to us as we continue our reflections is the unfinished masterpiece, the *Pieta Rondanini*.

We are told that Michelangelo carved this Pieta out of an earlier work which he destroyed. The earlier project seems to have been closer to the high Renaissance style which we usually recognize as the artist's hallmark. A strong, unattached right arm, compared with the rest of the Pieta, is evidence of the change. The form of the *Rondanini* piece is vertical, with the naked body of Christ resting almost full-length against the body of his Mother. At the base, they both merge into the remnants of the marble of the previous statue.

As we contemplate the *Pieta Rondanini*, we see what has been called a "contorted, expressionistic work," even an "unfinishable" work. Everything has begun, but nothing has been completed: not the left arm of the Mother, holding a dead son against her own unfinished body; not the arms, the body or the face of the son. The marble bears the rough marks of the sculptor's hammer; only the legs of the son seem to bear the signs of an initial polishing.

In the last thirty years of his life, Michelangelo seemed to be grappling with art concepts and art forms which reflected a deeper, inner change. He seemed to be seeking ways to move beyond the humanism and naturalism of the High Renaissance period. Only in the human figure did he shows signs of his earlier style. In the *Pieta Rondanini*, however, all of this is changed. If one were not informed

69

Agnes Cunningham

in advance, one would not identify this unfinished work as one to be credited to Michelangelo.

Emotion and feeling are characteristics of the Pieta image. Artists have vied with one another in their attempts to express the sorrow of Mary in taking the body of her dead son into her arms. Words like: melancholy, sorrow, compassion, anguish, torture, desolation, have been used to describe the Mother's sentiments. We also find evidences of "noble restraint," "the nobility of suffering," "the nobility of peace." The *Pieta Rondanini*, unlike other works of art by Michelangelo, reflects the artist's move from a portrayal of the idealized human body as a symbol of faith to the depiction of "human brokenness."

In choosing the Pieta as a subject of reflection, we are actually directing our contemplation to the Mother of Sorrows. This image of Mary emerged, in the fourteenth century, in relation to that of Jesus portrayed as the Man of Sorrows. The Pieta brought to the level of popular piety the reality of Christ, wounded for our sins, and of Mary, burdened with compassion for her dead son.

Devotion to the "seven sorrows" (originally, five) of the Blessed Virgin Mary spread, especially in Germany and the Low Countries. In art, Mary was portrayed with her heart pierced by seven swords, representing her spiritual martyrdom realized through compassion with the sufferings of Jesus in his Passion and death. These swords represented the seven great sorrows of Mary's life: Simeon's prophetic words (Lk. 2:34-35); the flight into Egypt (Mt.

Mary, Mother of Sorrows

2:13-15); the loss of Jesus in the temple (Lk. 2:48); the carrying of the cross; the Crucifixion (Jn. 19:25); the taking down from the Cross and the burial. In the Pieta, Catholic piety found a fitting object of devotion to the Mother of Sorrows.

THE MESSAGE

The message transmitted by the unfinished Pieta of Michelangelo begins with the artist himself. It has been suggested that this masterpiece reflects a concern which preoccupied Michelangelo for a great many years in later life. Some authors express this preoccupation as that of a Catholic influenced, to some extent, by the Reformation. Although he never ceased to be a Catholic, he was haunted, in a sense, by thoughts of sin and death, of salvation, of the "radical tension" that exists between nature and grace. In other words, Michelangelo struggled with the mystery of God—and of a God made man who suffered and died for us. In the *Pieta Rondanini*, Michelangelo invites us, also, to face this mystery—one he has been unable to grasp —or express—except in brokenness and incompleteness.

The second "word" of the message comes to us from the Catholic tradition of devotion to the Mother of Sorrows symbolized in the image. While there are some evidences of devotion to the *Mater dolorosa* in the patristic era, it was only with the Middle Ages and into modern times that this devotion took shape. One reason for reticence in the

Agnes Cunningham

age of the Early Church Fathers seems to have resulted from Origen's (+ A.D. 254) erroneous interpretation of Simeon's words to Mary. According to Origen, the "sword" that was to pierce Mary's heart was a "sword of infidelity and doubt" in regard to her son and his mission. A sixth-century liturgical poem offers the first defense of Mary's fidelity through the time of her suffering.

From the sixth century on, devotion to the sorrowing, suffering Mother developed throughout Christendom: in the East, first of all; then, in the West. The Pieta became a preferred representation of the *Mater dolorosa*, beginning in the fourteenth century, in France, Spain, Germany and Holland. The multiple representations of the Pieta, in painting and sculpture, attest to the vigor of Catholic devotion to Mary portrayed in this image.

An underlying spiritual theology leads us to a third element in the message transmitted by the Pieta. Devotion to the Mother whose heart was pierced by the "sword" of seven sorrows enables us to understand Mary's share in the suffering of her son and Savior. Her suffering can be understood as the birth-pangs of spiritual motherhood, a theme discussed earlier in this book. Mary's compassion with and for Jesus is an indication of the place she is to hold in our spiritual life. Mary's compassion becomes a mirror of the Passion of Jesus Christ. We cannot contemplate her without being drawn to him. If we are faithful to the fruit of this contemplation, we shall be led away from sin. Contemplation of the sufferings of the Savior must lead, inevitably,

Mary, Mother of Sorrows

to reflection on his dignity and on our own call to share trinitarian life eternally.

Still another message comes to us from the *Pieta Rondanini*. This, as we have seen, is an *unfinished* work. The statue, however, is hailed as a masterpiece, even in this incomplete state. Knowing what to do about its execution and the artist's intentions, we can discern a certain symbolic statement in it. This Pieta represents, from an artistic point of view, a transitional stage, between one style and another. It thus becomes the invitation to make a unique contribution to human endeavor in those areas where progress, growth and development are necessary and appropriate.

As the reflection of an inner journey of faith on the part of the artist, the unfinished statue of the Pieta speaks to all of us who are *in via*, "on the way." The artist's experience, further, reminds us of the fact that the devotional life of the Church, like every ecclesial reality, follows the ebb and flow of times, seasons, climates, cultures and civilizations. Devotion to the Mother of Sorrows emerged and developed in the Church in an age when the image of a suffering Mother and son was a source of inspiration and consolation to the faithful. Once discovered, the devotion has continued to speak to the Church. Its time has not passed. The Pieta remains "unfinished."

We might want to ask what difference the unfinished state of the *Pieta Rondanini* makes—or has made—to the transmission of the theme addressed by the artists of the

73

Agnes Cunningham

Middle Ages and the Renaissance. The absence of any other figures results in a certain stark quality in the scene. When John the Evangelist and Mary Magdalene are included, the artist has wanted to include, symbolically, repentant love and innocent love or, as Jean Guitton has pointed out, "the entire mystery of Redemption."

In the unfinished Pieta, the rigidity of death is eliminated by the curve and position of Christ's *torso*. The almost faceless head of Christ cries out to those who seek God in mystery and struggle to find him. Without arms, the body of Mary's son seems almost limp and yet it remains upright. The dead Christ seems to have been reduced to utter helplessness, still it is not because of his Mother's physical strength that he continues to defy the law of gravity. The Mother, too, overwhelmed with grief seems rooted in an attitude of acceptance, submission and peace. The lines of an inner tranquility are already etched on her face. The suffering of the Mother of Sorrows speaks to us as a chastening corrective in a world where excesses of emotionalism can distort even religious fervor and devotion.

The overall message of the *Pieta Rondanini*, in the last analysis, is a plea. The Mother and son, almost one in the vertical lines of the sculpture, call to us to look at the consequences of sin and evil. They invite us to compassion, that is—as the Latin root of the word indicates—to "suffer with" them. They urge us to acknowledge that the world has been redeemed. They ask us to remember that there is still need for each one of us to "fill up what is lacking in the sufferings of Christ for the sake of his body, the Church" (Col. 1:24).

THE TEACHING

The early Christians living in an age of persecution honored Christ with a title that touched their lives directly. Jesus Christ was the "First Martyr." Mary has also been acknowledged as martyr, in a spiritual way, because of compassion with the sufferings of her son. The teachings of the Church on Mary's "spiritual martyrdom" are based especially on texts in the gospels according to John (19:25) and Luke (2:35). The theme of Mary as the New Eve (cf. Gen. 3:15-16) and her association with the Servant of Yahweh, "Man of Sorrows" (cf. Is. 53:1-12) are also foundational to this image. The sufferings of Mary, as derived in Church teachings from the Scriptures, include her pain in the rejections and misunderstanding experienced by her son; the interior sacrifice of consent to the death of her son for our sins; the intensity of her sorrow when she stood on Calvary.

The sufferings of Mary were never the object of a formal dogmatic declaration by the Church. Nevertheless, there is a body of teachings that direct our understanding of the mystery of Mary's participation in the redemptive work of her son. St. Ambrose (+A.D. 397), bishop of Milan, pictured Mary beneath the cross, enduring with courage her awareness of the Redemption. Between the sixth and the tenth centuries, this image of Mary was developed in the East, although the West had to wait until the eleventh and twelfth centuries for a comparable growth. In the thirteenth century, the hymn, *Stabat Mater*, of uncertain authorship, was probably composed.

Devotion to the Mother (or Virgin) of Sorrows developed in the Church through the inclusion in the liturgical calendar of feasts and offices in honor of Mary under this title. In the twentieth century, Pope Pius XI (1923) affirmed Mary's role in the Redemption wrought by Christ. About ten years later (1933-1934), he proclaimed her share in the redemptive work of Christ at Bethlehem as well as on Calvary. In the Litany of Loreto, Mary is hailed as "Queen of martyrs." In the revised Roman calendar, the Latin Church continues to celebrate the Feast of Mary's Sorrows on September 15.

Explicit teaching on what is entailed in devotion to the Mother of Sorrows began, especially, with Pope Leo XIII. Pope Leo affirmed that Mary's sufferings began at the Annunciation. Beneath the Cross of Calvary, she stood with the Second Adam as the New Eve. She united her own sorrow to the Redeemer's sufferings and thus became Mother of all the sons of Adam. Thanks to the impetus given by Pope Leo XIII to this devotion, the Mother of Sorrows has retained an important place in the devotional and liturgical life of the Church.

The sufferings of Mary, as portrayed in the image of the Pieta, are characterized by certain virtues. The first and highest of these was Mary's love. Because of her perfect

Mary, Mother of Sorrows

love as a mother, Mary was particularly sensitive to the sufferings of her son. She experienced them almost as if they were her own. A second characteristic of Mary's suffering was her faithful constancy. Neither interiorly nor exteriorly did she ever falter in her acceptance of God's will and her patient endurance under trial. St. Bonaventure and other medieval theologians praised Mary's courage and self-mastery, her obedience and interior acquiescence to God's plan and the place she was called to take in it.

The Church, on occasion, has had to intervene in the instance of exaggerated notions of Marian piety that are incompatible with Catholic tradition and teaching. This was the case in relation to an extreme and erroneous interpretation of the text in John (19:25), which portrayed Mary as fainting away in the arms of the holy women present with her on Calvary or swooning in the arms of St. John. Some writers would have atttributed to Mary a type of "spasm" at the moment when she met Jesus carrying his cross to Calvary. Artists hastened to depict such scenes in all their realism, frequently with unpleasant or undesirable results. At the beginning of the sixteenth century, the Church rejected a petition to institute a feast in honor of "Our Lady of the Spasm"!

There is a final aspect of Mary's sufferings which must be addressed, especially in light of the Pieta as an image that introduces a corrective balance to exaggerated expressions of devotion to the Mother of Sorrows. Here, I am referring to certain texts or locutions ("sayings") allegedly communicated by Mary within the context of private rev-

77

elations or apparitions. At times, the tone of these communications might easily lead one to think that the Virgin is actually, at this time, experiencing pain because of the sinfulness of human beings, especially, of her children, the followers of her son. The mood of these sayings is frequently pessimistic, judgmental, threatening.

It is not possible to discuss here the delicate, difficult or, even, ambiguous nature of private revelations. Certainly, the life of the Church has been enriched by many of them, declared authentic and not contrary to Catholic doctrine after serious, prolonged examination. The devotional life of the Church and the personal prayer life of believers has been enhanced by contributions from great saints who stand in the mystical tradition of Christian spirituality.

In the presence of such phenomena, two criteria can guide us in our response or reaction to "directives" or "recommendations" that come to us from this realm. The first, of course, is the message of the gospel. Whatever is in harmony with the written word of God, as preserved and transmitted in the Church, can only be for our good. The second is the teaching of the Church regarding true and authentic Catholic devotion to the Mother of God. An image like the Pieta is of inestimable assistance to us at a time of such discernment.

SIGNIFICANCE

The Pieta speaks to us in a direct and immediate way of the lasting significance of martyrdom in the Church.

Mary, Mother of Sorrows

This is not an idle statement. In the Dogmatic Constitution on the Church, *Lumen gentium*, 42, the Fathers of Vatican II identified the charism of martyrdom as the highest gift, after charity or love, given by the Spirit to the Church in every age. The expression of love given by Jesus in dying for us is the model of the one who lays down his or her life for the Lord and for others. There will always be Christians called "to give this greatest testimony of love to all," as there always have been "from the beginning." The Church considers martyrdom "the highest gift and supreme test of love."

The word, *martyr*, like so many other words in the vocabulary of Christian spirituality and theology, derives from a Greek word. Its meaning, simply, is: *witness*. The martyr bears witness to faith in Jesus Christ as Risen Lord and Savior. Before Constantine bestowed his favor on Christianity, in the early fourth century, to become a Christian meant to expect to be a martyr. The accounts of the heorism of women, men and children in the presence of persecutors, torture, wild beasts, ridicule and every sort of wile to lure them from the Christian faith are well known. We are awed and inspired by the courage of the martyrs. We are in wonder at the evidence of the extraordinary graces with which God sustained and encouraged them.

Ignatius of Antioch (+ c. A.D. 110) claimed to be "God's wheat"; he prayed to be ground by the "teeth of wild beasts" so as to become "Christ's pure bread." Tertullian proclaimed that "the blood of martyrs" is seed for the

Church. Vatican II acknowledges that this gift is not given to everyone. We are all admonished, however, to "be prepared to confess Christ" before others and "to follow him along the way of the cross." The Church, *Lumen gentium* affirms, never lacks persecutions. In many parts of the world, today, Christians are being imprisoned, tortured and put to death only because they are Christian. Those of us who are not called to a "martyrdom of blood" must still bear witness to our faith in Jesus Christ through a lifestyle that identifies us as his disciples. Perhaps our "white martyrdom" will be more subtle; it need not be any less difficult.

The Pieta also speaks to us of the meaning of suffering in human life. Suffering has been described as a mystery. Insofar as it always entails some diminishment of normal human existence, it is spoken of as a poverty or an evil. In and through Christ, human suffering has been transformed. From Jesus Christ and his sorrowing Mother, we learn that suffering, which marks every human life—at one time or another, in one way or another—need not be without value. St. Paul tells us that "the sufferings of the present" are "as nothing compared with the glory to be revealed in us" (Rom. 8:18). He assures us that we who "have shared much in the sufferings of Christ" will share in his consolation (2 Cor. 1:5). He yearns "to know how to share in" the sufferings of Christ "by being formed into the pattern of his death" (Phil. 3:10). Paul rejoices because he can "fill up what is lacking in the sufferings of Christ for the sake of his body, the Church" (Col. 1:24).

Still, suffering—our own or the suffering of someone whose life touches ours—remains a strong challenge for us. The suffering of the innocent, in particular, is a scandal to us. Faith and devotion to the Mother of Sorrows do not resolve the problem of suffering for the believer; neither do they remove the pain and distress we experience because of suffering. We can hope to learn from the Pieta the lesson of patient endurance. Perhaps we can come to be inspired by persons who tell us that their lives have been enriched beyond imagining by the suffering they have had to bear. We can try to understand what our attitude toward and in suffering ought to be through Paul's words: "It is God's will that you grow in holiness" (1 Thess. 4:3).

"To be a Catholic means to carry the whole world in our heart." This is true, in a special way, where suffering is a reality. It often seems all we can do to be present to the suffering of an individual neighbor, friend or family member. The pain and anguish of one person are multiplied and extended to global dimensions in our experience through the printed and electronic media. At times, the awareness of the mutilation, exploitation and oppression of peoples through violence, cruelty and injustice becomes a burden on our minds and hearts. We are tempted to depersonalize the message, to distance ourselves from the pain, to "seek refuge" in prayer for the world. The unfinished *Pieta Rondanini* refuses to let us escape or close our eyes to the harsh phenomenon of suffering in humanity. We must try, in some concrete manner, to find a way to alleviate and lessen at least one person's suffering, every day.

From the Pieta, too, we can learn to pray for the world and for those who suffer in a manner that is not an escape. Intercessory prayer has been an essential part of the tradition of Christian prayer from the earliest ages. This is a form of prayer that has frequently been criticized or ridiculed as unworthy of informed or "enlightened" Christians. The gospel accounts tell another story. Jesus urged us to *ask that we might receive.* He gave us the example of intercessory prayer and taught us to ask the Father for our "daily bread." He encouraged us to pray with confidence (Mt. 7:9) and persistence (Lk. 18:3). He encouraged us to pray that the rigors of temptation and trial be mitigated (Mt. 24:20). Intercessory prayer, inspired by compassion, love, courage and obedience (Heb. 5:8) is the prayer we must offer for all who suffer in the Church and throughout the world. It is we who must contribute to the completion of the unfinished Pieta.

V. A Woman For All Seasons

THE IMAGE

A great sign appeared in the sky, a woman clothed with the sun, with the moon under her feet, and on her head a crown of twelve stars. Because she was with child, she wailed aloud in pain and she labored to give birth. . . . She gave birth to a son—a boy destined to shepherd all the nations with an iron rod. Her child was caught up to God and to his throne. The woman herself fled into the desert, where a special place had been prepared for her by God; there she was taken care of for twelve hundred and sixty days (Rev. 12:1-2, 5-6).

THE Book of Revelation has long been looked upon as one of the most difficult books in the Bible. The opening verses of Chapter 12 constitute one of the most difficult passages in Revelation. Who is this woman? What is the meaning of her encounter with the dragon?—an incident omitted from the passage quoted above. Who is the child? What does the desert represent? How are we to interpret the length of the woman's stay in the desert? More to the point, perhaps, what is the relation between the Woman of the Apocalypse—as she has been traditionally called—and Mary, about whom we are concerned in this book?

It is not possible nor, for our purposes, necessary to attempt to unravel the difficulties in the opening pericope of Revelation 12. What will be of greater interest to us will be to examine this "woman clothed with the sun" as a possible image of Mary: Ever-Virgin, *Theotokos, Mother of God, Mother of the Church, Mother of Sorrows.* Is the woman of Revelation 12 truly Mary, "A Woman for All Seasons"?

The Woman is described graphically enough to be familiar to us. How many paintings of the Blessed Virgin Mary depict her as such a woman! Artists have employed every technique of human ingenuity to portray the radiance of garments suffused with sunlight. She stands bare-footed on the moon—usually a graceful crescent-arc. The twelve stars about her head are now a crown, now a halo, now a shining *aureola.* The statues that have adorned our churches and homes or the holy cards that have served as bookmarks show us this woman. It is, perhaps, difficult for us to think of her as other than the Mother of Jesus! If the *Theotokos* has represented the Mother of God to Eastern Christians throughout the ages, the Woman of Revelation 12 has served that purpose for Catholics in the West.

From the earliest ages of Christianity, the Woman of Revelation 12 was understood to be a type or figure of God's people. The representation of Israel as a woman was common in the Old Testament. Continuity with this custom was only one evidence of the integration into Christian thought of ideas brought by Jewish converts to Christianity. The "people of God" meant, at times, the Israel of the Old Testament; at times, the new Israel of the New Testament. Some writers understood that the "people of God" included the faithful of both Covenants.

From the fourth century on, Christian writers began applying the image of Revelation to Our Lady. The first explicit reference was made by a fifth-century disciple of St. Augustine, Quodvultdeus. He wrote, "None of you is ignorant of the fact that the dragon was the devil. The woman signified the Virgin Mary...." Later writers developed this theme, seeking in the details of the scriptural text a deeper, allegorical meaning. Christ was the sun that clothed Our Lady; the twelve Apostles were the crown of stars about her head.

St. Bernard (+1193), who has been called the Doctor of Our Lady in the Medieval period, acknowledged the entire tradition in his sermon, *In signum magnum*. He reads the whole biblical passage in an ecclesiological sense, but adds that there is "no inconvenience in applying it to Mary." Bernard's reading of the text generally prevailed in later centuries. Theologians and other scholars who sought to interpret the Scriptures read a primary, or literal, meaning and a secondary, or "mystical" meaning of the passage. In some instances, the first level applied to the Church and the second, to Mary. At times, the interpretation was reversed. When the Woman was understood in an ecclesiological sense, she became, for some writers, a symbol of the Church in glory at the end of time. The close association of Mary and the Church in the text of Revelation came to be generally accepted. Cardinal Newman affirmed that the Holy Spirit intended the Woman to be an image of the Church because there existed, first of all, a blessed Virgin Mary.

However we tend to read the passage in Revelation 12, we cannot deny that the image of the Woman presented there has spoken to generations of Catholics in a Marian sense. One has only to examine the story of devotion to Mary, for example, in every Indo-American or Latin American country. Each nation has its preferred *"Virgen,"* a portrayal of Mary that has assumed historical, religious and, sometimes, political importance for the people of the country. In every instance, one discovers in the image held in veneration a Woman whose description echoes that of Revelation 12. There are, certainly, signs of the national or regional culture incorporated into the artist's work. Perhaps the unique character of a Madonna would be found in an instrument or a piece of fruit in her hands. The names of the Virgin differ, too, from country to country, but, basically, we find the Woman: Holy Mary—"clothed with the sun, with the moon under her feet, and on her head a crown of twelve stars."

If we attribute a Marian symbolism to the Woman of Revelation 12, we must go one step further. We must recognize in this image of Mary the overtones of other images we have reflected on in earlier chapters. Most striking are the similarities between this biblical image of Mary and the Ever-Virgin of Guadalupe. Beyond any specific reference, however, we find in the Woman of Revelation 12 an image of Mary presented as a Mother for all peoples and a "woman for all seasons." The message is one of significance for our age.

THE MESSAGE

The Woman in Revelation 12 proclaims a triple message to us who look to her as an image of the Virgin Mary, Mother of God. That message can be expressed in three significant words: liberation, celebration, exaltation.

Mary proclaims a message of *liberation* to her children. In order to recognize this message, we have to read chapter twelve of the Book of Revelation in its entirety. The dragon who sweeps stars from the sky and stands "ready to devour [the] child when it should be born" is not unlike the serpent who is to wage war with the offspring of "the woman" (cf. Gen. 3:15). In fact, the text identifies the dragon and "the ancient serpent"...."the devil or Satan, the seducer of the whole world" (Revelation 12:9). Cast down by Michael and his angels, the dragon is "hurled down to earth" where he again takes up battle against the woman. In Apocalyptic style, we see the woman carried to safety on the wings of an eagle, rescued by the earth itself from a torrent spewed out of the dragon's mouth, and, finally, fully rescued from her enemy. The woman's child had been previously "caught up to God and to his throne." The "rest of her offspring," still pursued by the dragon, are called to strive through observance of the commandments and through bearing witness to Jesus to come to final deliverance.

The woman's liberation from the dragon is a promise and guarantee of our freedom from the forces of sin and evil. The Church prays daily to Mary, asking that she pray for us "now and at the hour of our death." The "hour of death" is every hour in which we are beset by temptation and trial, as well as that "last hour" when we prepare to leave this life. As we conclude the reading of Revelation 12, we know that the Christian life remains a struggle. We also know that liberation has been achieved by the woman and her child. Chapter twelve, in the last analysis, is the story of a triumph. Because we acknowledge the woman as Mary, our Mother, we can be confident that the liberation can also, one day, be ours. The conditions are simple. Mary is there as model and guide to assist us.

The second word of the message is *celebration*. This aspect of the message may not be immediately or directly obvious. To understand it, we must reflect briefly on the Christology that comes to us from Liberation Theology.

One of the criticisms of Liberation Christology is that it is incomplete. It leaves us with a suffering Savior who is crucified, who dies and who is buried. The Risen Christ has been markedly absent from the Christology that has been articulated in Liberation Theology. Dialogue within the theological community will undoubtedly address this alleged weakness. However, there is a deeper level of reality involved here—one which has, no doubt, contributed to the theological position just described.

Theologians tell us that developments in Christology are reflected in Mariology. The change from a "high" Christology, which largely prevailed before Vatican II, was accompanied by a "high" Mariology. In other words, emphasis on Christ's divinity went hand-in-hand with emphasis on the special prerogatives bestowed on Mary. So too, the "low" Christology that has characterized theological discourse since the close of Vatican II has seen the development of a "low" Mariology. In this perspective, the accent on Christ's human nature has been reflected in the attention given in Mariology to the human qualities and "ordinariness" of the Mother of Jesus.

This is not the case with Liberation Christology. The focus on Christ in the countries of South America leads us to Gethsemane and Calvary. It is the Crucified Lord who is honored and revered. The devotions of the people are directed to the Cross. Holy Week and Good Friday are the high points of the liturgical year. The Risen Christ is still to be discovered by the vast majority of believers. The Resurrection is a feast that has still to be granted its rightful place.

In contrast, Mary is honored in her glory. Her feasts are

the occasion of celebration. Her shrines and altars are adorned with flowers, banners and votive offerings. Pilgrimages bring crowds together in her name. In every instance, she is honored under titles and in images that recall the Woman of Revelation 12. She is the Immaculate Conception and the Virgin assumed into heaven in one and the same portrayal. Her presence is a cause and a summons to celebrate her triumph over sin and death. Music and dancing are the order of the day.

The contrast between devotion to Christ and the veneration shown to Mary reflects a simple fact: the experience of a people. The native peoples of South America, and the countries themselves, have still to know a "resurrection" on the world scene. This is as true of the Church as it is of society in general. Liberation theology envisions such a "resurrection." How can the Risen Christ be brought to these people? The answer, again, lies in the experience of a people.

In the far-flung reaches of the vast territories that lie far from the cities, for example, in the *pampas* of Argentina, the father of a family is often absent. Perhaps he is a *gaucho* who rides with the great herds of cattle which he guards for a wealthy, absent owner miles away in Buenos Aires. Perhaps he, himself, must travel hundreds of miles to find work to provide for the family. In the absence of the father, it is the mother who keeps his memory alive for the children. It is also the mother who announces the return of the father. It is the mother whose joy at the father's approaching arrival prepares the feast,

A Woman For All Seasons

sets the tone of rejoicing in the home and calls the entire family to celebrate.

South American theologians tell us that Mary, the Mother, never ceases to call her daughters and sons to celebrate the coming of the Lord. They are convinced that celebration of the Virgin will lead, eventually, to awareness that Jesus Christ, too, has given us reason to rejoice. The triumphant Mother will lead her children, without fail, to the son who has triumphed over all evil and every form of death. The Mother assumed body and soul into heaven will make known, in time, the resurrection of Jesus Christ, her son.

The third word of the message communicated by the Woman of Revelation 12 is: *exaltation*. This aspect is consequent upon the two previous words, liberation and celebration. She who has been freed from the snares of the dragon is honored as blessed among women and summoned by God to be Mother and Queen. The Woman of Revelation 12 has been adopted as the image of the Virgin Mary: preserved sinless; celebrated as triumphant over the dragon; taken up into heavenly glory to be with her God for all eternity. The Church has affirmed in her official teaching the full realization of Christ's saving work in Mary.

THE TEACHING

The teachings of the Church most in harmony with the image of Mary portrayed in Revelation 12 can be found

91

in the dogmas of the Immaculate Conception and the Assumption.

By the Immaculate Conception of the Virgin Mary, the Catholic Church teaches that Mary was preserved free from all stain of original sin from the first moment of her existence. Mary was conceived as all other human beings are; she was preserved sinless through the merits of Jesus Christ, by reason of a special grace and a singular privilege.

The Immaculate Conception of the Blessed Virgin Mary was proclaimed a dogma of the Catholic faith by Pope Pius IX, on December 8, 1854. The word, "dogma," comes from the Greek and means, "what seems right." The definition of a dogma means that a teaching of the Church is to be believed with "divine and Catholic" faith. A dogma is taught expressly in the ordinary magisterium (teaching office) of the Church, by the Pope speaking *ex cathedra* or by a council. It is declared to be divinely revealed, contained in the word of God and belonging to the Apostolic Tradition. Denial of a dogma constitutes heresy. A dogma need not always have been regarded as such, but may come to be recognized in time, as the original message of revelation is clarified under the guidance of the Holy Spirit in the Church.

In the case of the dogma of the Immaculate Conception, the scriptural evidence is found in an implicit manner. This means that selected biblical texts, when interpreted by the Church in the light of what Vatican II called a "further and full revelation," do point to Mary's preservation from all sinfulness at every moment of her life. The most important scriptural passage for this dogma is Genesis 3:15: "I will put enmity between you and the woman, and between your seed and her seed; he shall bruise your head, and you shall bruise his heel." A first reading of this text leads us to identify the "woman" as Eve, with the entire human race as her "seed." It is because the text is one that points unfailingly to the coming of a Messiah and his work of salvation that the "woman" can be taken to refer to Mary. This reading becomes more certain in the light of the Eve-Mary, Adam-Christ parallel which it invokes.

A number of Scripture scholars do not hesitate to identify Mary as the woman in Genesis 3:15. This meaning of these words is affirmed by the salutation of the angel (Lk. 1:28) and the greeting of Elizabeth (Lk. 1:42) to Mary. These three passages, when taken within the context of the living tradition of the Church, bring together the serpent in the garden of Eden, the fullness of Mary's grace, her union with Jesus as Mother and as new Eve and the promise of redemption made to our first parents. This implicit scriptural foundation is none the less certain, particularly when we recognize that the progressive witness of the Fathers of the Church supports it.

Prior to the Council of Nicaea (A.D. 325), affirmations about Mary were always made in terms of her relationship with Christ. Explicit teaching of an "immaculate conception" do not appear in this period. The blessings and

Agnes Cunningham

graces attributed to Mary are the result of her unique place in the life of Christ. Writers after Nicaea are more direct in their statements that point toward a fuller understanding of Mary's holiness and freedom from sin. However, some early theologians, including St. Augustine and, later, St. Thomas, had reservations about Mary's preservation from Original Sin. That, they claimed, was the prerogative of Christ alone. Between the fifth and the thirteenth centuries, belief in Mary's freedom from all sin and from every fault became more clearly expressed. The studies of biblical scholars and theologians contributed, in subsequent centuries, to the clarification necessary to find in the teaching of the Church a solid ground for the definition of the dogma in 1854.

Before a century had elapsed, that is, on November 1, 1950, another Pope defined another Marian dogma: the Assumption. Pius XII, in an Apostolic Constitution entitled *Munificentissimus Deus,* proclaimed that Mary, Mother of God, had been assumed, body and soul, "into heavenly glory." Centuries before the promulgation of this dogma, Catholic belief and devotion had honored Mary's glorification in heaven through prayers, hymns and poetry. From the fifth century on, the feast of Mary's "birthday into heaven" was celebrated by Greek and, eventually, by Latin Christians. In the East, the feast commemorated the Dormition or "falling asleep" of the Virgin. In the West, emphasis was, rather, on the Assumption. The difference in focus resulted from uncertainty as to whether or not Mary actually died. There is no certain answer to this question; it is generally held that she did experience death, but not the consequences of death before she was "taken up" by the power of God.

The Scriptural evidences for the dogma of the Assumption, like those for the Immaculate Conception, are foundational and implicit, rather than clearly stated. In his definition, Pope Pius XII again cited the text from Genesis 3:15, along with others: Revelation 12; Luke 1:28 and 42. Historically, Mary's image as the New Eve has been the inspiration for exegetical and theological understandings of the Word of God that have contributed to the development of the Church's teaching on Mary and the singular privileges bestowed on her by God as Mother of Jesus Christ, true God and true man.

The dogma of the Assumption of Mary, like that of her Immaculate Conception, leaves many questions unanswered. Our intellects and human curiosity would like to know details that neither Scripture nor Tradition addresses. The cumulative weight of Catholic faith and scholarship over the centuries has led to a reading of the biblical texts not always agreed upon by other Christians. The official teaching of the Church both challenges and supports our acceptance of what has been revealed as "divine and Catholic teaching." In the definition and promulgation of the Marian dogmas, the Church urges us to recognize that the graces granted to Mary are, in the last analysis, affirmations about Jesus Christ and his saving work. They also speak to us about God's loving will for the whole Church and the holiness to which all of us are called. The "woman clothed with the sun" stands on the horizons of our hope as a promise of what we are one day to share.

SIGNIFICANCE

When Pius IX defined the dogma of the Immaculate Conception of the Blessed Virgin Mary in 1854, reactions in the Catholic world were largely positive. The subsequent apparitions of Mary, in 1858, to Bernadette Soubirous at Lourdes in France confirmed these reactions. Outside the Catholic Church, however, the mood was negative. The Christian churches of the Reformation did not agree that Mary was different from the rest of the human race. The Orthodox rejected the concept of Original Sin underlying the dogma.

In 1950, the situation was somewhat different. When Pius XII proclaimed the dogma of Mary's Assumption, negative reactions came, first of all, from within the Catholic Church. These reactions were not a sign of non-acceptance of the teaching. Rather, the timeliness of a dogmatic definition, particularly one concerning Mary, was questioned. The definition was seen as a possible obstacle to new developments in ecumenism. However, there was also a strong positive reaction among Catholics. In the wake of two world wars and the devastation of the concentration camps, the dogma affirmed human dignity, the

A Woman For All Seasons

value of human life and the glorious resurrection to which the human body is destined. Non-Catholic Christian churches of the West were negative, for both ecumenical and doctrinal reasons. On the contrary, the Orthodox were in agreement with a teaching that had been an important element in their doctrinal, liturgical and devotional traditions from earliest times.

What significance do these dogmas have today in the life of the Church? This question can be answered from several different perspectives. When we consider the proclamation of the Immaculate Conception in its historical context, we realize that it was only one of a series of important Marian "events" that occurred during the nineteenth century. A rich flowering of devotion to Mary was reflected in the number of religious "Marian" Congregations that came into existence from the beginning of the 1800's. It has been estimated that approximately seven hundred congregations for women, all expressing dedication to Mary in their title, were founded in the nineteenth and early twentieth centuries.

Another phenomenon especially particular to the nineteenth century was the number of apparitions of the Virgin that were recorded, beginning with the appearance of Mary to Catherine Labouré in 1930. By the end of the first third of the twentieth century, La Salette (1846), Lourdes (1858), Pontmain (1871), Knock (1879), Fatima (1917), Beauraing and Banneux (1933) had taken their places with Rue du Bac and the Miraculous Medal. The prudence of the Church in cases of alleged apparitions results in great caution and, often, in rejection of the claim of the visionaries. Nevertheless, these events always seem to revitalize a response to the gospel call to prayer, penance and a deepening of faith, frequently in an atmosphere of extreme rationalism. In the Church at large, whatever reception may be granted to or withheld from reports of an apparition of Our Lady, there results a deepened conviction that a loving, caring Mother never ceases to pray for us to her Divine Son.

A third Marian event of note in the nineteenth century was the rediscovery, in 1842, of a manuscript entitled, "Treatise on True Devotion to the Blessed Virgin," by Grignion de Montfort (+ 1716), one of the masters of the French School of Spirituality of the seventeenth century. His little work knew almost immediate success. It was translated into about fifty languages and within a short period of time had reached its three-hundredth edition. The encyclical on the motherhood of Mary (*Ad diem illum,* 1904) was written by Pope Pius X after he had read de Montfort's work.

New developments in Marian devotion and spirituality continued to mark the nineteenth century. Through the efforts of Pope Leo XIII, the rosary was adopted as a special expression of Marian prayer. In 1826, the movement of the "Living Rosary" which has been recently restored, was founded by Pauline Jaricot. In 1846, Mary, under the title of the Immaculate Conception, was named patroness

A Woman For All Seasons

of the United States. With the second half of the nineteenth century, serious efforts to provide a sound theological foundation to Marian doctrine and devotion can be identified.

The intentions of the Fathers of Vatican II, along with the writings of Pope Paul VI and Pope John Paul II, assure a continuity of fidelity to the authentic teaching of the Church regarding the Mother of Jesus Christ. We are the beneficiaries of this rich heritage of the last two-hundred years. The Immaculate Conception has been named patroness of our country. We are challenged to seek inspiration and guidance in this dogma for understanding God's mercy to us insofar as we are sinners and God's call to us to grow in knowledge, love and discipleship of Jesus Christ, son of God and son of Mary.

I have called the Woman of Revelation 12 a "woman for all peoples, a woman for all seasons." It is this image of Mary that has most strikingly represented the Assumption, expressed as a dogma by Pope Pius XII, after centuries of Catholic belief and devotion. What significance does this teaching have for us, today? The Virgin assumed "into heavenly glory" seems to speak to us in at least three ways.

In the first place, the image of Mary as the Woman of Revelation 12 truly exemplifies Mary as "the eschatological icon of the Church." Our reflections on images of Mary throughout this book have demonstrated again and again her relationship to the Church, her part, as Vatican II stated, in the mystery of the Church. Mary is a member of the Church, but she is also Mother, guide and model of the Body of Christ.

In Mary, everything that God willed a human person to be has been fulfilled: faith and discipleship; obedience and response to the will of God; fidelity, courage, commitment and patient endurance. In every circumstance made known to us in Scripture and through the Apostolic Tradition, Mary appears as the beloved daughter of God the Father, the chosen Mother of God the Son, the faithful spouse of God the Holy Spirit. What Mary is and has become the entire Church is called to be.

The Assumption of the Virgin is a symbol of that taking up into glory that Christ wills for all his Church. The Church is to be the spotless bride of Christ. He wills "to present to himself a glorious Church, holy and immaculate, without stain or wrinkle or anything of that sort" (Eph. 5:27). At the End-Time, the Church is to be ready for that presentation. Contemplating Mary as her "eschatological icon," the Church will enter more deeply into the mystery of an on-going share in an "assumption" that has already begun, through the grace of Christ, her lover, bridegroom and head.

The Assumption carries significance for us, secondarily, in what the dogma affirms regarding the value of human life. This was certainly one of the implications of the teaching, at the time of the definition, when the horrors of war and racial genocide had seared our consciousness. In a world where sin in all its forms of evil and error seems too often to prevail or, at least, to obstruct goodness and justice, Mary's Assumption transmits a corrective and a counter argument.

In "A Marian Creed" published after his death, Neal M. Flanagan, O.S.M., professed his faith in the meaning of Mary's Assumption for us today. Like Christ's resurrection, he tells us, it gives us proof and hope that "love is truly stronger than death." The stories of heroic virtue and amazing examples of Christian love that continue to emerge from the concentration camps confirm this reality, already announced in the Old Testament: "For stern as death is love,...Deep waters cannot quench love, nor floods sweep it away" (Sg. 8:6, 7). Death—however Mary experienced that mystery—was for her what it is for us: the passage to a new and fuller life. The dogma of the Assumption calls us to a hope that carries us through the darkest experiences of this life.

Finally, Mary in her Assumption gloriously proclaims a truth that speaks to the experience of women today. Many women writers express distress when confronted repeatedly by male images and names for God. The second creation account (Genesis 2) tells us that human beings, created in the image of God, are both male and female. The Old Testament reveals God to us in images and titles that reflect both feminine and masculine qualities.

Jesus told the Samaritan woman whom he met at Jacob's well (Jn. 4) that "God is spirit." Anthropomorphic language meets the limitations of our human minds and the categories of our thoughts. Still, it is difficult to move beyond these limits, when they provide the predominant—or the only—way of speaking to or about God. The Virgin of the Assumption becomes, once again, an icon: this time, an icon that leads us into the mystery of the feminine "otherness" of God. Neal Flanagan has perceived rightly that Mary's son bears witness to God incarnate in the masculinity of Jesus, while Mary herself recalls to us that God can be found in feminine beauty. Mary assumed into heavenly glory points to the "feminine face of God." In contemplating the mystery of Mary's Assumption, we may be able to move toward more inclusive religious language and images in fidelity to the essential Revelation of God in Jesus Christ.

Appendix I

O N March 25, 1987, Pope John Paul II published an Encyclical Letter on "the Blessed Virgin Mary in the Life of the Church." The title of this document is: "The Mother of the Redeemer" *(Redemptoris Mater)*. In the encyclical, the Pope announced a Marian Year to be observed in the Church from Pentecost Sunday (June 7, 1987) to the feast of the Assumption (August 15, 1988). A number of feasts and observances have been planned throughout the Catholic world in view of celebrating the Marian Year. Until recently, however, little has been done to encourage the reading or the study of the Pope's encyclical. What is an encyclical? Why is there hesitancy or indifference regarding such a document? Why did Pope John Paul II write this encyclical and proclaim this Marian Year? What does the Pope have to say about Mary that has not already been said in the teaching of the Church in the past?

THE ENCYCLICAL

An encyclical can be defined as a letter sent by the Pope to the entire Church and even beyond the Church to the whole world. The encyclical is, ordinarily, addressed to the bishops ("Venerable Brothers") and the other members

of the Church ("dear Sons and Daughters"). The salutation usually includes a greeting ("Health and the Apostolic
Blessing"). An encyclical letter does not, ordinarily, reflect
the full teaching power of the Pope. In other words, an
encyclical is not, necessarily, infallible. Much would depend on the subject of the encyclical and, particularly, on
the Pope's expressed intent to teach official Catholic doctrine on a matter of faith and morals, as visible head of
the Church *("ex cathedra")*. Since an encyclical always is
a "teaching moment" in the life of the Church, it is wise
for Catholics to be informed of the contents of any such
"letter" from the Pope.

Why, then, are encyclicals so infrequently read by the
general Catholic population? There are several reasons
which come to mind. In the first place, copies of encyclicals
are not always readily available. They are published
simultaneously (or nearly so) in multiple languages, in
booklet form, usually by the National Bishops' Conference.
Sometimes, a diocesan newspaper or agency will make
copies available. However, the vast majority of people seem
to have to depend on the secular press for a summary of
the encyclical's contents and significant quotations from
the document.

Once a copy of the encyclical is available, other difficulties present themselves. The format and language of the
encyclical are not familiar to us. This is a formal document, written according to a predetermined form and style.
The vocabulary reflects classical theological discourse. The

Appendix I

original language of the encyclical, more often than not, is Latin. Occasionally, if a Pope is fluent in Italian or French, a first draft may be prepared in one of those languages, with a Latin translation following almost immediately.

The question of language is a major one where the reading of any ecclesiastical document is concerned. Frequently, translations are hurriedly done. Sometimes, the person is either unaware or insensitive to the nuances of a language, as it is spoken in various geographical or cultural settings. For example, English differs from Ireland to Jamaica, from South Africa to the United States. Within the United States, there are sometimes notable differences in expressions and vocabulary between Maine and Tennessee, Chicago and Dallas, Haight Asbury and Martha's Vineyard. Most people want to read texts that reflect the language *they* speak. Encyclicals are not written—or translated—to fulfill that desire.

Another aspect of the language question is the matter of exclusive or sexist language often found in an ecclesiastical document. This point is particularly germane to the reception of a papal encyclical in the United States, because of widespread sensitivity of women, as a result of the feminist movement. The absence of inclusive language from an encyclical or other communication from Rome is not necessarily due to close-mindedness or misogyny. More often than not it is the consequence of a translator's lack of knowledge or awareness of currents that prevail in a given culture. Latin, like some other languages, is either naturally gender inclusive or provides in its syntax and vocabulary for inclusion of both women and men. This is not a suggestion that there is no need for improvement or growth in the area of sensitivity to women in religious, theological or canonical language. Rather, it is important to recognize all the possible factors that may come to bear on what seems to be a discriminating statement.

One other factor, at times, comes into play to influence response to a papal encyclical. That is a reaction based on presuppositions regarding the "hidden agenda" that may lie under the stated purpose of the document. This is the case, especially, at those times when a Pope's theological or philosophical positions have been clearly stated and are generally known. The same may be said about presuppositions regarding the contents of the document, when individuals anticipate a too "liberal" message, on the one hand, or "nothing new," on the other.

These and, perhaps, other reasons which I have overlooked have an impact on the response to and acceptance of any written communication from the Pope. Unfortunately, important developments in the life of the Church can be bypassed by such real or imagined difficulties. Two striking examples of this occurred in relation to the Apostolic Exhortation on religious life, *Evangelica testificatio*, by Pope Paul VI and that same Pope's other Apostolic Exhortation on renewal of devotion to Mary, *Marialis cultus*.

Appendix I

It was only with time that widespread recognition of the importance and uniquely rich quality of these two documents was realized.

THE CONTENTS

The encyclical, "The Mother of the Redeemer," consists of an Introduction, three major Parts and a Conclusion. In the Introduction, the Pope announces his intention to reflect on Mary's role "in the mystery of Christ and on her active and exemplary presence in the life of the Church." The Pope's reflection is based on the teachings of the Second Vatican Council, especially on the Dogmatic Constitution on the Church, *Lumen gentium*. Part I is devoted to "Mary in the Mystery of Christ." Part II is entitled: "The Mother of God at the Centre [*sic*] of the Pilgrim Church." Part III addresses Mary's "Maternal Mediation." The Conclusion is a brief statement that directs our vision toward the future, assuring us of Mary's presence to assist the whole people of God in their journey.

Why did Pope John Paul II write this document at this particular time? The Pope's devotion to Mary is well known. A number of reasons for the timing of the encyclical can be found in the text, itself. The first, and most obvious, is to call the entire Catholic world to begin its preparation for the celebration of entrance into the third millennium of Christianity in the year 2000 (3). A second reason

Agnes Cunningham

is to recognize Mary's place in the history of salvation: "the Church has constantly been aware that *Mary appeared* on the horizon of *salvation history before Christ*" (3).

Two other anniversaries are singled out for special consideration. One is the "Millennium of the Baptism of Saint Vladimir, Grand Duke of Kiev (988)," which will take place during the Marian Year. Here, we note the Pope's particular ecumenical concern and his keen interest in Eastern Christianity, both Orthodox and Catholic. He urges union in prayer "repeating and confirming with the Council [Vatican II] those sentiments of joy and comfort that 'the Easterners... with ardent emotion and devout mind concur in reverencing the Mother of God, ever Virgin' " (50).

The other anniversary is the twelfth centenary of the Second Ecumenical Council of Nicaea (787). At that council, the controversy regarding sacred images was resolved. According to the decision of the council, "there could be exposed for the veneration of the faithful, together with the Cross, also images of the Mother of God, of the angels and of the saints, in churches and houses and at the roadside" (33).

The proclamation of a Marian Year (49) draws attention to other reasons for the encyclical. As Robert Moynihan pointed out in the May 31, 1987, issue of the *National Catholic Register*, the Pope calls us, at this time of moving toward the end of the Second Millennium of Christianity, to prayer for Christian Unity, to a deeper spiritual life and to greater knowledge and love of Mary.

Appendix I

One of the most interesting aspects of the encyclical is the list of sources on which Pope John Paul II draws for inspiration and support of his teaching. The Second Vatican Council is a major source: the Dogmatic Constitution on the Church *(Lumen gentium)*, the Pastoral Constitution on the Church in the Modern World *(Gaudium et spes)*, the Dogmatic Constitution on Divine Revelation *(Dei Verbum)*, the Decree on Ecumenism *(Unitatio redintegratio)*. The writings of Pope Paul VI and those of earlier Pontiffs—St. Leo the Great, Leo XIII, Pius IX, Pius X, Pius XII—are cited. Texts from earlier councils or from Roman documents also figure as sources. Perhaps the richest theological references are to the Scriptures themselves, to the writings of the Fathers of the Early Church and to some medieval theologians. The Pope has also known how to draw on the traditions of Christian art and poetry—specifically on Dante (10); Ephrem, Harp of the Holy Spirit and the Ethiopian traditions (31); the rich and varied adaptations of the *Theotokos* image (33).

THE THEOLOGY

There is a subtle indication of the theological orientation taken by Pope John Paul II in his choice of the titles he chooses for Mary in his encyclical. In general, these reflect the classic teachings of the Church: Blessed Virgin Mary, Mother of God, Mother of Jesus, Virgin Mother, Mother of Christ. Others echo the Litany of Loreto or other Marian prayers or invocations: Mary of Nazareth, Star of the Sea, Morning Star, Queen of the Universe, Daughter of Zion. Titles we have come to know from the Scriptures or Tradition are included in the Pope's reflections. He gives special emphasis to the *Theotokos*, cherished by Eastern Christians. In one section of the encyclical (33), he specifies the multiple ways in which this tradition has been developed, giving particular mention to two icons: Our Lady of Vladimir and the Virgin of the Cenacle.

Although the Pope affirms Mary's universal motherhood, he does not use the title, Mother of the Church, or refer to Pope Paul VI's proclamation of that image until late in the document (47). This point will be important for a discussion of the present Pope's teaching on the relationship which exists between Mary and the Church.

The theological foundations of Mariology, as presented in the encyclical, are clearly indicated as the Trinity and the Incarnation. Mary's relationship to Christ and to the Church is the consequence of "the love of the Father, the mission of the Son, the gift of the Spirit" (1). As Mother of the Son of God, Mary "is also the favourite daughter of the Father and the temple of the Holy Spirit" (9). In the mystery of the Incarnation, Christ and Mary are "indissolubly joined." He is the Church's Lord and Head; she prefigured the Church's condition as spouse and mother when she spoke "the first *fiat* of the New Covenant" (1).

The Pope's reflection on Mary, Mother of the Redeemer, is developed through three theological themes. These can be expressed as her pilgrimage of faith, her entrance into the mysteries of Christ's life and her presence in the Church.

MARY'S PILGRIMAGE

The theme of Mary's pilgrimage is announced early in the document (1). The theme is based on *Lumen gentium*, 58 and has a threefold dimension. Mary's journey is *personal*, that is, it is her own; it is *ecclesial*, because it reveals how the Church is to journey toward the End-Time and her meeting with the Lord; it is *universal*, since Mary stands, as Mother, at the heart of all creation.

Mary's journey is her own. It is a pilgrimage and its essential quality is faith. Mary advanced along the path she was to travel as virgin and as mother. In her way of being virgin and mother, we discern the "interior history" manifested in any pilgrimage of faith: the story of her relationship with God, her openness to grace, her response to a call. Mary's journey began at the moment of the Annunciation (8), when the words, "full of grace" were first addressed to her. The journey was externalized in Mary's visit to Elizabeth, which became the occasion for another stage in the development of her faith.

Still another milepost on Mary's journey was marked by the words of Simeon. Pope John Paul II describes this scene as a "second Annunciation," shedding new light on her understanding of what she was being called to by God and what was envisioned for the son she was to bear (16). At this point, Mary's awareness and insight added new depth to her faith. She began to realize that her motherhood was to be "mysterious and sorrowful." She learned that her faith was to be lived out in obedience, "at the side of the suffering Saviour."

The great moments of Mary's personal history, as recorded in the Scriptures, tend to make us forget the years of her persevering faithfulness at Nazareth. The Pope insists on the importance of this time of hiddenness, of day-to-day living by which she advanced step-by-step along her pilgrimage. The years of "union with her Son" were the years of journeying in faith toward the Cross and what seemed to be the denial of all her hopes. On Calvary, Mary shared "through faith" in what the Pope calls the "shocking mystery" of Christ's *kenosis*.

The quality and depth of Mary's faith are affirmed in gospel scenes from which Mary is absent as well as in those where her presence and action are described. Whenever Jesus blesses those who believe, he is first of all blessing his Mother and her faith. When he seems to disregard her or her words, it was only to respond to her faith. Pope John Paul II quotes the words given by Dante to St. Bernard to speak of Mary: "daughter of your Son" (10). If Mary's personal journey of faith can be traced from the Annunciation to the Assumption, it is because she learned to advance in her pilgrimage by living with Jesus as he grew in wisdom and grace (Lk. 2:52).

Mary's journey was not hers alone. In fact, we might

Appendix I

say that the *leit-motiv* of the encyclical is found in the ecclesial significance of her pilgrimage of faith. The Pope calls attention to the fact that the liturgy for the Feast of the Immaculate Conception acknowledges Mary as the "Church's own beginning." He states, further, that the Annunciation marks both the "fullness of time" fixed by the Father for the Incarnation of the Word as well as the "hidden beginning of the Church's journey." Furthermore, the Church proceeds on her pilgrimage, following the path traveled first of all by Mary. In going before, Mary becomes a figure or model of a Church that is to walk in faith, hope and love, in union with Christ. Mary is the model of a Church that is to be a virgin in her fidelity and a mother to children born of water and the Spirit.

One of the important aspects of the Church's journey, according to Pope John Paul II, is the "sign of ecumenism." This is a special characteristic of our age. Christians have heard Christ's prayer that his disciples be one as he is one with the Father. There is increasingly widespread recognition that division among Christians is truly a scandal. The Pope urges all Christians to deepen the "obedience of faith" which Mary lived on her pilgrimage. This obedience is needed by individuals as well as by ecclesial bodies. The Pope maintains that unity can be realized only on condition that it is based on the unity of faith.

In questions of Christian unity as in other ecclesial questions, Mary is the model of those who desire to do what Jesus tells them, following Mary's counsel, as at Cana.

Agnes Cunningham

Christians who hope and strive to promote unity among Christians are already walking together in a shared pilgrimage of faith. The Pope signals as a "hopeful sign" the growing agreement between other Christian Churches and the Catholic Church regarding Mary's importance in the life and mission of Jesus Christ, true God and true man. This is, of course, particularly the case with the "Orthodox Church and the ancient Churches of the East." He suggests that all Christians look to Mary as our "common Mother" who is the first of many "witnesses to faith in the one Lord." From her, we can learn to sing what the Pope calls the " '*Magnificat*' of the pilgrim Church."

The *universal* character of Mary's pilgrimage of faith is highlighted by Pope John Paul II in several instances in the text of the encyclical. In the first instance, he states that Mary's "exceptional" journey is a "point of constant reference" not only for the Church, but for each one of us individually, for the communities to which we belong and even, for peoples, nations and all humanity. The extent of Mary's pilgrimage is such that our ability to measure its range is defied. Mary's faith-journey no longer belongs to her alone, the Pope declares. It belongs to all who still walk in faith (6).

In a similar way, Mary's "fullness of grace" is a spiritual blessing which the Pope sees as intended for all people. It clearly carries a dimension of "universality" (7). Mary is not absent from that design by which all humankind is called to "share in the divine nature." God's plan for the

114

Appendix I

"divinization" of human beings has been realized in Christ. The Pope speaks of the "humanization" of God's Son to match the historical conditions that come to bear on the "divinization" of all persons. The transformation of human beings and, indeed, of all human history which the Pope envisions is the fulfillment of that universally significant "pilgrimage of faith" which Mary pursued on earth.

In his efforts to emphasize the universal dimension of Mary's journey, Pope John Paul II turns for inspiration to the anthem sung by the Church at the conclusion of the Liturgy of the Hours during Advent: "Assist your people who have fallen yet strive to rise again" (*Alma Redemptoris Mater*). These words are the words of "every individual, every community,...nations and peoples,...the generations and epochs of human history." The transformation that takes place "from 'falling' to 'rising' " occurs within every individual's personal journey and in all the events of every human being's history (52).

Thus, Mary is "deeply rooted" in the history of all humankind. The progress realized in any area of human endeavor—science, the arts, technology—calls to mind the final vision in which all things are to be brought to God in and through Christ (cf. Eph. 1:10). There is a special importance of this eschatological vision for women in the present, the Pope claims. He urges further study on the "unique relationship" between femininity and the Mother of the Redeemer. He identifies the qualities that Mary helps the Church to see in all women: "the self-offering totality of love; the strength that is capable of bearing the greatest sorrows; limitless fidelity and tireless devotion to work; the ability to combine penetrating intuition with words of support and encouragement" (46).

MARY'S SHARE IN THE MYSTERIES OF CHRIST

We can speak of Mary's journey of faith as an ever-deeper entrance into the mysteries of the life of her son, Jesus Christ. Indeed, we can trace Mary's advancing steps along her pilgrim way through the successive, progressive revelation of the mysteries of the life of the Lord. Pope John Paul II identifies these "moments" or "events" in Mary's experience. This concept of *entrance into the mysteries of Christ* is the unifying theme of Part Two of the encyclical.

The Pope states that it was through the event of the Annunciation that Mary was "definitively *introduced into the mystery of Christ*" (8). This "mystery" seems to refer to the totality of the Christ-Event as God's plan of salvation for the world. This first "entrance" affirmed Mary's place in God's salvific design. The mystery is summed up in the words of the angelic salutaton: *full of grace.*

The Pope develops this phrase, relating it to the text in Ephesians (1:3) in which Paul proclaims the universality of God's plan. The fullness of grace attributed to Mary, then, is a spiritual blessing which has meaning for all women and men, even though it pertains to Mary "in a

116

Appendix I

special and exceptional degree" (8). In a sense, Mary is given a new name, when she is saluted as "full of grace." Through this grace, she is chosen by the Father and the Son. A seed of holiness is sown within her, and she is entrusted to the Spirit of holiness. Fullness of grace in Mary has implications for time and for eternity.

The Annuciation, in a more specific way, is the event by which Mary enters into the mystery of the Incarnation of the Word of God. We are reminded here of the spiritual doctrine of Cardinal de Bérulle, Jean-Jacques Olier and other great men and women who founded and developed the French School of Spirituality of the seventeenth century. The "mysteries" or "states" of the Incarnate Word constituted an essential element of this spiritual tradition. For Bérulle, especially, the Christian life was to be a life in which both contemplation and apostolic service were important. Christians were to live in union with Jesus Christ through entrance into his mysteries.

With an emphasis on Mary's entrance into the mysteries of *Christ*, the visit to Elizabeth becomes, in the encyclical, another aspect of the mystery of the Incarnation. The Annunciation is the moment for which all of creation has waited. In that sense, it is a "culminating moment," as the Pope points out. It is also the point at which Mary's pilgrimage of faith begins. The hopes of prophets and patriarchs find a certain realization in that moment. Through her *fiat*, she agrees to treasure these hopes as they are carried to fulfillment in the life of her Child.

Agnes Cunningham

Pope John Paul II perceives the event of the Annunciation and the words, "full of grace," as a kind of wellspring from which meaning was to flow into every stage along Mary's faith-journey. In this light, he interprets the words of Simeon, the visit of the Magi, the flight into Egypt. Other events, too, even when marked by their own unique significance, stand in the light of that initial event. The Pope's way of expressing this is to present the Annunciation, at another level, as Mary's initiation into the "radical 'newness' of God's self-revelation" (17).

The next mystery into which Mary enters is that of the hidden life of Jesus at Nazareth. During those years, Mary lived in close, daily contact with her son. Through faith, she was in daily, constant contact with the mystery of God. Her faith perdured from year to year as Jesus grew in wisdom, age and grace, apparently the son of the local carpenter (Mt. 13:55). Pope John Paul II compares Mary's share in the mystery of the hidden years to the dark night—the "night of faith"—described by St. John of the Cross (17). Her experience of this mystery of Jesus' life was extended and prolonged, even as he began his public ministry. To the extent that the Lord was not fully recognized by others, to that extent, there was a "hidden" quality in the exercise of his ministry.

At the foot of the Cross, Mary enters into still another of the mysteries of her son's life. This time, it is the mystery of Christ's self-emptying. Mary's blessedness in believing, proclaimed by Elizabeth, "reaches its full meaning" on

118

Appendix I

Calvary. In that mystery, Simeon's words were realized: Jesus became a "sign of contradiction"; Mary's heart was pierced by the sword of sorrow (18). Entrance into the mystery of Christ's *kenosis* is, for Mary, entrance into the mystery of the Redemption. Here, Christ is the New Adam; here, Mary is the New Eve. Mary's obedience and faith reversed what Eve had effected.

The mystery into which Mary entered on Calvary, at a still deeper level, is the "Redeemer's Paschal Mystery." This moment marks the end of a movement begun at Cana. In the earlier event, Mary contributed to the start of Christ's "messianic activity." She desired the beginning of that activity. She spoke as the "spokeswoman of her Son's will" (21). Her faith in Jesus called forth the manifestation of his power and the faith of his disciples.

In a somewhat surprising development, Pope John Paul II discusses at length the nature of Mary's *mediation*, a role which was not included in the teaching of the Second Vatican Council. The Pope understands that the human need recognized by Mary at Cana symbolized the mediating intervention which brought that need into the sphere (the "radius") of Christ's salvific mission. On that occasion, Mary chose to be the one who was to stand "in the middle"—between the multiple needs of human beings and her son. The event at Cana announced Mary's mediating role—which is not that of a "mediatrix," the Pope insists, but that of a mother. Mary's mediation is "maternal" in character. It is directed solely towards Christ and is exercised only to bring about a revelation of his saving power (22).

The entire third Part of the Encyclical (38-50) is devoted to what the Pope calls, "Maternal Mediation." The section opens with a firm affirmation of Jesus Christ as the one and only mediator between God and us. Mary's mediation, according to the Pope, is "mediation in Christ." What does this mean?

Mary's mediation can be spoken of as "saving influences" which flow from the superabundant merits of Jesus Christ. Her mediation is maternal, as the event at Cana indicates; it is also a *shared* mediation, that is, it is exercised in cooperation with Christ's unique mediation, as Vatican II suggested (*Lumen gentium*, 62). Thus, Mary's mediation is understood by the Church to be a sharing in the grace of Christ. Mary, clearly, has a subordinate role in the work of salvation, although her role is, at the same time, "special and extraordinary." She is the one who is to lead us to the one Mediator who is Christ.

When we speak of Mary's mediation, we must recognize the relation of this quality to her maternity. At the foot of the Cross, Mary's motherhood was transformed to embrace all those for whom her son had suffered and died. Her desire to see all human beings brought to Christ impelled her to cooperate with him in his saving mission. With his death, her mediation, subordinate to his, assumed universality. Her mediation is one of intercession; it "continues in the history of the Church and the world." It contributes to the union that exists between the pilgrim Church on earth and the Communion of Saints. Because of her unceasing care for the Church, the Pope tells us that Mary can be properly addressed as Advocate, Auxiliatrix, Adjutrix and Mediatrix (40). Her "motherhood" must be considered *"in the dimension of the Kingdom of God and in the radius of the fatherhood of God"* (20).

MARY'S PRESENCE IN THE CHURCH

The Pope's apparent reluctance to invoke Mary under the title, Mother of the Church, has already been referred to above. That does not mean that the concept of her universal and spiritual motherhood or acknowledgment of it is in any way denied or presented as inappropriate or misplaced. The words to Mary and John on Calvary are a "testament." They clearly establish Mary as mother of every single individual and of the entire human race. She is mother "of the members of Christ." Her "motherhood of the Church is the reflection and extension of her motherhood of the Son of God" (24).

Pope John Paul II's discussion of the way in which Mary as Mother relates to the Church is extremely nuanced. Mary's share in the mystery of Christ was effected in order that she might become his Mother, the Holy Mother of God. Through the Church, she remains in that mystery as the "woman" of Genesis (3:15) and as the "woman" of the Apocalypse (Rev. 12:1). As Mother, Mary becomes "present in the mystery of the Church." This quality of Mary's presence is the characteristic of Mary's motherhood emphasized by the Pope.

Mary resides at the center of the Church as a maternal presence. She is present to all the People of God, as they continue their journey of faith. Mary is present as one who believed, as one who has gone before on the pilgrim way, as one who entered in a unique way into the mystery of Christ. Mary is present to the Church as a mirror, reflecting the great things God has done, holding them before us for our contemplation and acclaim. Mary is present in the Church as a model of faith and persevering prayer.

Mary's presence in the Church is a presence of witness to the mystery of Jesus. Pope John Paul II tells us that, from the earliest ages of Christianity, the Church " 'looked at' Mary through Jesus" and " 'looked at' Jesus through Mary" (26). Mary is present in the Church not only as one who believed, but as the *first to believe.* Mary "belongs" to the mystery of the Church, just as she belongs to the mystery of Christ. Her faith is a special legacy hidden in the heart of the Church.

There are other dimensions to Mary's unique presence in the Church. One of these is her presence in the work and mission of the Church for the proclamation and building of God's Reign. The manifestation of this apostolic presence of Mary is found in individuals and families, in parishes, religious communities and diocesan churches. It is reflected wherever nations or peoples come together in faith and piety, to observe and celebrate the traditions of

Appendix I

Christianity. Shrines and centers of devotion suggest that one might speak of a "geography" of faith and devotion to Mary.

One of the signs of Mary's presence in and with the pilgrim Church is what the Pope calls the " '*Magnificat*' of the pilgrim Church." Initially, this canticle was a profession of Mary's faith and her response to God's Word in her life. In the life of the Church, the *Magnificat* proclaims Christ's triumph over sin and the truth about a God who does great things. It affirms the Church's commitment to bring light and truth to human life. It professes her love and preference for the poor. In her faithful echoing of Mary's *Magnificat*, the Church acknowledges her duty to safeguard the poor and her option to serve the poor.

In the *Magnificat*, the Church learns daily the Christian meaning of liberation and freedom. Mary is present in the Church, finally, as the "most perfect image" of freedom and liberation. The full meaning of the mission to which the Church is called is brought to light through the presence of Mary.

In her divine maternity, Mary is present as a figure and "permanent model" for the Church. The Church is a mother when she accepts God's word faithfully. She is a mother in bringing children to new life, through preaching and baptism. Mary, as Mother, is "*at the service of the mystery of the Incarnation.*" The Church, as mother, serves the "*mystery of adoption to sonship* [*sic*] through grace."

Mary is also present in the mystery of the Church as a

model of faith, hope and charity. More than that, she "cooperates" in realizing the motherhood of the Church through her own spiritual motherhood, "born from the heart of the Paschal Mystery of the Redeemer of the world" (44).

In his comments on Pope Paul VI's proclamation of Mary as Mother of the Church, the present Pontiff explains his understanding of the title. Mary, he states, "is present in the Church as the Mother of Christ." She is also present as the "Mother whom Christ, in the mystery of the Redemption, gave to humanity in the person of the Apostle John" (47). This is Mary's motherhood "in the Spirit." By it, she embraces everyone *in* and *through* the Church. Finally, Mary is present in the Church as Mother of the Redeemer. With her children, she engages in the struggles that mark the pilgrimage of all those who walk in faith.

CONCLUDING REFLECTIONS

The encyclical, *Redemptoris Mater*, merits more than I have been able to do in the preceding presentation. There are many sections that call for prayerful reading and reflective study. An examination of the documents from which Pope John Paul II has drawn would also be rewarding, as an exercise that might contribute to an ongoing renewal of devotion to Mary.

In many ways, the encyclical is an affirmation, once again, of traditional Catholic teaching about Mary. It is

Appendix I

also more than that. There is a development beyond the Marian doctrine enunciated by the Second Council of the Vatican. There is also a development beyond the teaching of Pope Paul VI on devotion to Mary.

Two major contributions to new theological understandings about Mary deserve particular mention, especially, since they did not receive sufficient attention in the material presented above. The first is the strong historical dimension that can be traced through the encyclical. The universal character of Mary's pilgrimage of faith has resulted, effectively, in her presence in and to the Church and the world at every critical junction of human history. This fact becomes increasingly clear, as one reads and re-reads the document thoughtfully and attentively. The implications of this phenomenon for our own age could result in creative approaches in efforts to renew authentic devotion to Mary.

The second interesting contribution is Pope John Paul II's reflection on the relationship that results from the fact that *the essence of motherhood concerns the person* (45). From this affirmation, the Pope proceeds to address the *Marian dimension of the life of Christ's disciples.* The paradigm chosen in this section is the relationship that the Pope suggests could have developed between Mary and John as a consequence of their response to Christ's words on the Cross. Here, we can recognize Pope John Paul II's dominant interest in the human person and in the quality of interpersonal relationships. His reflections invite us to apply to our reflections on Mary the principles and learnings

Agnes Cunningham

derived from studies in the human sciences. We are reminded of Pope Paul VI's insistence on the need for an anthropological dimension to effective renewal of devotion
to Mary.

It is too early to foresee what reception this encyclical
will receive in the Church at large. Nor is it possible to
predict what impact it will have on Marian doctrine and
devotion in Catholic faith and piety. An enrichment of
mind and heart will surely come to those who are willing
to grant the document more than a superficial reading.

In the last analysis, it would seem that *The Mother of
the Redeemer* could well be a challenging document for
Mariologists, Scripture scholars and theologians to study,
long after the Marian Year it announced has ended. With
Marialis cultus, Redemptoris Mater calls the Church to a
knowledge, love and veneration of Mary renewed, deepened and adapted to our time.

Appendix II: Devotion to Mary and Church Renewal

IF there is one thing to be learned from our reflections on the images of Mary presented in this book, it is that devotion to Mary has marked the life of the Church in multiple and diverse ways throughout the centuries. The multiplicity and diversity have been the result of the growth of the Church and the proclamation of the gospel to all peoples and nations, in every locality and culture throughout the world.

Devotion to Mary has frequently been a "barometer," indicating the state or condition of Catholic life and thought. From one point of view, it can be examined as the vehicle through which the mission of the Church has been transmitted. It has been the "instrument" by which the Church's integration or rejection of the efforts and achievements of human experience can be measured. Thus, we can affirm with Pope John Paul II, that the story of Mary's pilgrimage is the "story of all human beings." In a similar way, the history of devotion to Mary is closely related to the history of Church renewal. This can be demonstrated briefly.

At the very beginning of the Christian era, when the Infant Church still walked in the enthusiasm of what spiritual writers have called a "first fervor," devotion to Mary seems to have been non-existent. Mary was in the Church, but little, if any, explicit mention was made of her. Any expression of "devotion" would have seemed out of place in an era dominated by the memory of the Risen Lord and anticipation of his Second Coming.

The theological and spiritual insights of early second-century Apologists, like Justin Martyr, and anti-heretical writers, like Irenaeus of Lyons, contributed to a growing appreciation of Mary's significance for the Church's understanding of Christ. Following the diminishment of Christian integrity and devotedness which marked the Constantinian era, the proclamation of Mary's divine maternity at the Council of Ephesus (A.D. 431) brought about a renewal of faith in Catholic teaching based on the Creed proclaimed at Nicaea (A.D. 325). By the time the Council of Ephesus was held, Christians were already familiar with ideas of Mary's holiness, her perpetual virginity and her divine maternity. Mary was perceived as the New Eve and her relationship to the Church was affirmed in treatises by theologians like Ambrose of Milan. There had even been indications of belief in her "immaculate conception."

Between the Council of Ephesus and the Gregorian Reform (1050), little advance occurred in the development of a theology of Mary. This was the time for a flowering of Marian hymns and prayers, especially but not exclusively, among Eastern Christians. Between the beginning of

Appendix II

the eleventh century and the close of the Council of Trent, a number of Marian themes emerged. A general tendency toward decadence characterized the life of the Church during those centuries. Devotion to Mary found dramatic expression in the art and architecture of the Middle Ages. This was frequently inspired by rediscovered texts from the apocryphal gospels, in response to a popular interest in religious fantasy. Images of Mary honored at this time portrayed her as Queen, Advocate and Priestess.

The great cathedrals of France stand as a monument to Catholic faith and Marian piety, beginning in the twelfth and thirteenth centuries. In the images of Mary depicted at that time, we recognize the Mother who intercedes for her children; the Mother crowned by her son; the Virgin who stood alone in chapels and oratories where the faithful took refuge. When Mary was represented without Jesus, however, she frequently held the book of the gospels in her hands as a sign that her life was bound to the life of Christ.

The Middle Ages also saw devotion to Mary influenced by institutions and customs fostered by troubadours and knights. Shrines and pilgrimages, relics—at times questionable—and processions, practices of penance and votive offerings: all seemed to thrive, as believers vied with one another in witness to a faith subject to the exaggerations as well as the exaltation of the period. Devotion to Mary during these centuries was not conducive to promoting ecclesiastical renewal. Indeed, the need for "reform" in the

Church could be said to extend to all phases of Church life, including that of devotion to Mary. The Reformation, the Council of Trent and the Counter-Reformation were religious events that were to have lasting consequences.

In the history of the Church there are two "moments" in which renewal of Church life and renewal of devotion to Mary seem to have been mutually beneficial. The first of these times occurred after the Council of Trent, when instruction in the basic truths of Catholic faith and formation for living the Christian life were urgently needed. Response to Trent's call for interior renewal and external reform came in a striking manner from a movement that has come to be known as the French School of the seventeenth century.

Under the leadership of Pierre de Bérulle and a few lay companions, the design of a program of theological and spiritual formation was launched throughout France. The story of the French School cannot be recounted here. What is of importance to us, however, is its contribution to a development of Marian doctrine that was intimately related to an extraordinary renewal of the Church.

The central idea of the French School, as developed by Bérulle, was the theory of Christocentrism. In contrast to an "active Christocentrism" which envisages Christ as an "object" outside of us, Bérulle spoke of "mystical Christocentrism." By this, Bérulle understood that Christ is "one with us" and we are "one with him."

St. John Eudes, an early associate and companion of

Appendix II

Bérulle, is known for having built on the initial Marian devotion of the French School to develop a rich, full doctrine of Marian theology. In the French School, Mary is seen as the one person who perfectly lived "mystical Christocentrism." She "adhered" perfectly to Jesus; she was *one* with Jesus; she *identified* totally with Jesus. More than that, Mary is the model of "adherence" to Jesus and of identification with him. Through Mary—that is, through knowledge of her and contemplation on her life—we can learn how to arrive at union with Jesus.

St. John Eudes took the themes of Mary as the "temple" or "residence" of Jesus, as model of Christocentrism; as the means by which we can arrive at union with Jesus. From about 1643 on, we find these ideas suddenly appearing in the writings of John Eudes. Without changing the doctrine as it existed, he gave it a new form and a symbol: the heart. John Eudes' unique contribution consisted in a scientific, methodological, in-depth study of the theology of the heart of Mary.

What is meant by a "theology of the heart of Mary"? Without denying the reality of the physical, bodily heart of the Mother of God, John Eudes understood this organ in the biblical sense. The physical heart was the *symbol* of the whole person. Thus, it is possible to speak of the "spiritual" heart of Mary, which focuses on her love for Jesus and for God. It is also, according to John Eudes, possible to speak of the "divine" heart of Mary. By this, he understood that the entire Trinity dwelt in Mary in a unique way and that, in a particular manner, Jesus lived and reigned in Mary.

In the teaching of John Eudes, this way of speaking of a threefold dimension of Mary's heart accomplished two important things. First of all, it distinguished between the *symbol*—the physical heart—and the reality signified—the "spiritual" and the "divine" heart. Secondly, it pointed to the fact that to speak of the "heart of Mary" was to refer, above all, to her "divine heart."

What were the consequences of the teaching of St. John Eudes? History bears witness to the remarkable renewal of devotion to Mary that resulted from his doctrine and the propagation of this theology. Devotion to the heart of Mary began with St. John Eudes and has continued until today. Where there has been fidelity to Eudist teaching, the devotion has remained strong and healthy, rooted in the Scriptures and founded on the teaching of the Fathers of the Church and the great medieval theologians. Departure from the doctrine developed and taught by John Eudes has, unfortunately, had less happy results.

Renewal of devotion to Mary according to the tradition of the French School, as adapted and developed by St. John Eudes, contributed in a beneficient manner to renewal in the entire life of the Church. Emphasis on the "spiritual" or "divine" heart of Mary bore witness to the importance of interior renewal in the life of every individual, if the life of the Church were to be renewed. The importance of Scripture and the Apostolic Tradition in the instruction of the faithful and in the formation of the clergy was evidenced in the life of Mary, model of faith and discipleship. The ability to bring together both contemplation and apostolic action, as Mary did, provided encouragement, inspiration and a source of support for laity, religious and clergy.

An extraordinary revitalization of the Church took place in the Church as a result of the teachings of the French School. One essential element of those teachings derived from the renewal of Marian devotion fostered by the theology of St. John Edues. Echoes of this renewal, in its most faithful expressions, reached beyond the seventeenth century into the life of the Church. Even today, it is possible to identify the influence of the French School and the teachings of Bérulle and St. John Eudes in some of the best spiritual and theological achievements of the Church.

The second significant "moment" for an interplay between renewal of Marian devotion and ecclesiastical renewal occurred in another post-conciliar period. The Second Vatican Council, as we have seen, seemed at first to result in a diminishment of devotion to Mary. The teachings of the Council in the area of Mariology were the object of study by Mariologists, but aroused little interest or enthusiasm in other circles. However, the theology of the Council, like that of the French School, had retrieved strong elements of the biblical and Apostolic traditions. Mary was restored to her rightful place, *in* the Church and the affirmation of authentic Catholic teaching regarding her virginity and maternity provided a foundation on which Scripture scholars and theologians could build.

In the earlier sections of this book, we have seen how *Lumen gentium*, 8, along with the writings of Pope Paul VI and the recent encyclical of Pope John Paul II, have contributed to exciting and promising developments in Marian doctrine. The Church is encouraged to reflect on Mary in ways that are faithful to Catholic teaching, while being creatively adapted to the needs, insights and concerns of our age. From Pope Paul VI, we have learned that Catholic teaching about Mary must be characterized by trinitarian, christological and ecclesiological elements. Paul VI has also urged us to renew devotion to Mary according to biblical, liturgical, anthropological and ecumenical principles.

From Pope John Paul II, we have arrived at new insights regarding Mary as a woman of faith whose pilgrimage speaks to the experience of the entire Church and all of humanity. We have found her present at every significant moment in the history of her son's life as she has been present in and to the history of the Body of Christ and that of all human beings. In *Redemptoris Mater*, the present Pope also reaffirms in a new way the values expressed by Pope Paul VI, especially in *Marialis cultus:* trinitarian, christological and ecclesiological elements; biblical, liturgical, anthropological and ecumenical principles.

The renewal initiated in the Church following Vatican II has been implemented to a significant degree, although

Appendix II

much remains to be done in fidelity to the vision of the Council Fathers. Now that devotion to Mary is entering a new stage of renewal and development, it is time to identify areas where Marian doctrine and devotion can contribute to a more complete realization of the Council's goals.

This would entail an exploration of the significance of Mary for the Church's commitment to work for justice and peace; to service of and with the poor, the exploited, the abandoned, the homeless; for elimination of racism, sexism and all forms of oppression. It would encourage creative expressions of Marian devotion which take into account the diversity of culture, education, profession and nationality that enriches the unity of Catholic faith. The significance of Mary for "contemporary Catholics" will be realized to the extent that her life and the life of her son continue to call us to a life of faith and discipleship.

Suggested Readings

Brown, Raymond E., editor, et al. *Mary in the New Testament*. Philadelphia: Fortress Press, 1978.

Cameli, Louis J. *Mary's Journey*. New York: William H. Sadlier, Inc., 1982.

Graef, Hilda. Mary: *A History of Doctrine and Devotion*. New York: Sheed and Ward, 1963.

Greeley, Andrew M. *The Mary Myth*. New York: Seabury Press, 1977.

Houselander, Frances Caryll. *The Reed of God*. London: Sheed & Ward, 1944. Waldwick, New Jersey: Arena Books, 1978.

Jegen, Carol Frances, editor. *Mary According to Women*. Kansas City: Leaven Press, 1985.

Jelly, Frederick M., O.P. *Madonna: Mary in the Catholic Tradition*. Huntington: Our Sunday Visitor, Inc., 1986.

Noone, Patricia. *Mary for Today*. Chicago: Thomas More Press, 1977.

Agnes Cunningham

O'Carroll, Michael, CSSp. *Theotokos: A Theological Encyclopedia on the Blessed Virgin Mary.* Wilmington: Michael Glazier, Inc., 1986.

Pope Paul VI. *Mary—God's Mother and Ours.* Boston: St. Paul Editions, 1979.

Ruether, Rosemary Radford. *Mary: The Feminine Face of the Church.* Philadelphia: Westminster Press, 1977.

Smith, Jody Brant. *The Image of Guadalupe: Myth or Miracle?* Garden City: Image Books, 1984.

Tambasco, Anthony J., *What Are They Saying About Mary?* New York/Ramsey: Paulist Press, 1984.

Turner, Rita Crowley. *The Mary Dimension.* London: Sheed and Ward, 1985.

Warner, Marina. *Alone of All Her Sex: The Myth and Cult of the Virgin Mary.* New York: Alfred A. Knopf, Inc., 1976.